Social Media Marketing

A beginners guide to leveraging Facebook, Twitter, Instagram, and YouTube to become an influencer and grow your business!

© **Copyright 2019 - All rights reserved.**

The content contained within this book may not be reproduced, duplicated or transmitted without direct written permission from the author or the publisher.

Under no circumstances will any blame or legal responsibility be held against the publisher, or author, for any damages, reparation, or monetary loss due to the information contained within this book, either directly or indirectly.

Legal Notice:

This book is copyright protected. It is only for personal use. You cannot amend, distribute, sell, use, quote or paraphrase any part, or the content within this book, without the consent of the author or publisher.

Disclaimer Notice:

Please note the information contained within this document is for educational and entertainment purposes only. All effort has been executed to present accurate, up to date, reliable, complete information. No warranties of any kind are declared or implied. Readers acknowledge that the author is not engaging in the rendering of legal, financial, medical or professional advice. The content within this book has been derived from various sources. Please consult a licensed professional before attempting any techniques outlined in this book.

By reading this document, the reader agrees that under no circumstances is the author responsible for any losses, direct or indirect, that are incurred as a result of the use of information contained within this document, including, but not limited to, errors, omissions, or inaccuracies.

Table of Contents

Introduction 1

Chapter 1: What Is Social Media Marketing? 2

Chapter 2: The Importance of Social Media Marketing 7

Chapter 3: Creating Your Social Media Marketing Strategy 16

Chapter 4: Common Social Media Marketing Mistakes to Avoid 26

Chapter 5: How to Use Facebook to Grow Your Business 31

Chapter 6: How to Use Twitter to Grow Your Business 42

Chapter 7: How to Use YouTube to Grow Your Business 51

Chapter 8: How to Use Instagram to Grow Your Business 60

Chapter 9: Social Media Content Strategy 66

Chapter 10: Understanding Social Media Monitoring and Listening 74

Chapter 11: Growing Your Following on Social Media 84

Chapter 12: Running Ads on Social Media 91

Chapter 13: Tips and Tricks to Improve Your Social Media Conversion Rate 103

Chapter 14: Motivation from Businesses That Made It on Social Media 108

Chapter 15: The Future of Social Media Marketing - Trends to Follow 114

Chapter 16: Social Media Marketing - Why Most Businesses Fail .. 120

Chapter 17: Proven Secrets to Increase Your Brand's Visibility on Social Media 126

Conclusion 131

References 132

Introduction

Thank you for taking the time to read this book on social media marketing!

Throughout the following chapters we will discuss the different social media platforms, the pros and cons of each, and how to advertise on each of these platforms effectively.

You will also learn about choosing the right social media platforms for your particular business, the importance of creating a marketing plan, and also what exactly makes a good advertising campaign.

Whether you have an established business or are just starting out, this book will help you to gain a larger online following and increase your business through the strategic use of social media marketing! At the completion of this book you will be ready to launch a social media marketing campaign across different platforms and implement a variety of strategies such as paid advertisements and scheduled posts!

Thanks again for choosing this book, I hope you find it to be helpful!

Chapter 1: What Is Social Media Marketing?

Perhaps one of the greatest human weaknesses of today is that we are always in a hurry. As such, many individuals prefer fast food over cooking at home, they speed date, and some people even opt to use emojis rather than words. These behaviors display very well people's tendencies to be impatient, and this includes business owners. This impatience is clear in the way that many business owners utilize social media. Most people realize that social media marketing is important, however, they don't take the time to learn how to properly implement it. Instead, they dive right in and get frustrated when they don't get the desired results straight away.

With the fast pace in which the world is moving, such behaviors are understandable. Technology is moving at a such an increased rate that we never have time to fully adapt. New technologies are introduced every day; it is difficult to keep up with such abrupt changes. Consequently, you cannot be blamed for making irrational decisions when using social media to market your business. Unfortunately, adopting social media marketing without taking the time to comprehend how exactly it could help your business can do more harm than good.

Essentially, social media marketing is a smart method by which businesses can reach their customers and prospective clients. You should understand that your target audiences are already using social networks to connect with their friends and relatives. Today, these social platforms have made it possible for individuals to communicate with brands, too. For that reason, if your business has not utilized social media platforms to communicate with your customers, then you are on the losing end. There are many benefits that you can enjoy by using social media to create awareness about your brand and the products or services you offer. This is precisely what the most successful businesses in the digital world are doing.

So, what is social media marketing (SMM)? Simply stated, social media marketing refers to a form of internet marketing that makes use of social networking websites to act as a marketing tool. The main goal of social media networking is to create content to be shared by users to aid in increasing their brand awareness and the customer reach[1]. Basic activities that will be involved in this form of marketing include posting texts, uploading images and videos, and sharing content, which will, in turn, increase consumer engagement.

Marketing your business on social media might appear like a straightforward process. However, it is vital that you understand it is not just about uploading images and videos. There is more to social media marketing than just doing those basic things. Most business owners jump in to using social media marketing with the perception that by uploading engaging content, they can win customers over to their side. Prior to creating any campaigns on social media, it is imperative for one to reflect on their business goals. Also, you should have a strategy that you will use to promote your brand on social platforms. Without a plan, you will have no clear direction to follow. As a result, there is a likelihood that you will fail in the process.

Social media marketing will not only help you increase your reach, but it will also help you increase your sales leads. Using online social platforms will also provide yourself with an ideal way of getting feedback about your product or service. You

---

[1] "What is social media marketing (SMM)? - Definition from WhatIs.com." https://whatis.techtarget.com/definition/social-media-marketing-SMM. Accessed 26 May. 2019.

might also achieve your business marketing goals, including developing a good reputation about your brand, provide high quality customer service, drive traffic to your website, and ensure that people are always informed about new products or services you are yet to launch.

Since there are many social media platforms out there, you might be wondering which is the best platform for your business? Notable social media platforms include Facebook, Twitter, YouTube, Instagram, LinkedIn, and Pinterest. A huge mistake made by most businesses is that they think they should have an online presence on all these platforms. To be clear, it is not a must for you to have an online presence on all these networks. In fact, not all social pages will be suitable for your particular business. Choosing the right social network for your business will be discussed later in this book.

If you have been curious about growing your business, it must have crossed your mind that social media could be the best place to do it. Nonetheless, you probably have also wondered whether there is an ideal strategy that you should adopt in order to guarantee that you succeed in the process. Let's face it - many have tried social media marketing but have failed terribly. This is because there are mundane aspects of this form of marketing that you must understand.

Before you think about marketing your business on social media, you have to stop and ask yourself why you should be on social media in the first place. Why do you think your business needs to be on social media? Brainstorming answers to this question will help you better develop your social media business goals. In this case, you might be on social media either to promote products or to drive traffic to your business website. It could also be that you are on social media to serve your customers. Knowing why you need your business to have a social media presence guarantees that you set up the right social media strategy.

Aside from finding out why your business needs an online presence, you should also determine who your target market is. Knowing who your followers are will help you determine the best platform on which to share your content. For instance, if you are targeting the corporate working population, then it would be advisable to share content on LinkedIn rather than Facebook. Also, understanding your target audience will guide you in creating content that suits them. Varying content needs to be shared to the young population as compared to older adults. So, it is crucial that you know a lot about the individuals who might be interested in your products or services.

Now, as a part of ensuring that you share quality and informative content with your followers, you should know what to share. You shouldn't share something just because it excites you. Your business social media page needs to be distinct from your personal page. You have to keep in mind what your audience expects to read and watch. Basically, your audience will have a huge impact on what you will be sharing.

In addition to the above points, knowing where you will share your content is another crucial factor to bear in mind. Different people use social media for varying reasons. You ought to share your promotional messages on platforms that your audience regularly visits. Remember that you should focus on the few social media platforms that will guarantee brand growth for your particular business. Having an online presence on all social media networks will not necessarily help you. Stick to the chosen few, and promote your brand to the handful of pages where your target market is active.

Time is also a crucial factor in social media marketing. People access social media at different times of the day. So, you should find out how your target market uses social media. Your aim should be to schedule your posts during the times when your audience is most active. The advantage gained here is that you will have a wider reach.

Social media marketing is more than simply uploading content to social media platforms. To ensure that your business thrives, you must equip yourself with vital social media marketing knowledge. This book will delve into this knowledge over the following chapters to help you understand how to best utilize social media marketing in your business!

Chapter 2: The Importance of Social Media Marketing

Today, most businesses have made use of the internet to take advantage of social media marketing. Having an online presence has become an intrinsic part of any company. Most people use social media to communicate with their friends and family, so using these platforms to gain access to clients is a great way of reaching out to them. This is because businesses get to create an understanding of their brand, while simultaneously increasing traffic to their website. There are also other benefits that will accrue as a result of using social media marketing. This chapter aims to open your eyes to the realization that there are many positive aspects of using social platforms to market your business.

Driving Targeted Traffic

One of the main reasons why it is imperative to have an online presence is that most of your potential leads and customers are either on Facebook, Twitter, Instagram, or YouTube. Research shows that about 68 percent of American adults use Facebook. Also, 78 percent of youths aged 18-24 have Instagram accounts, and 45 percent of them have Twitter accounts.[2] These statistics make it evident that businesses can reach their leads through social media pages, and in order to do so, a business obviously has to have an online presence.

If you are running a new website, reaching out to potential clients on social media will certainly increase your website

---

[2] "18 Reasons Why Your Business NEEDS Social Media Marketing." https://www.contentfac.com/9-reasons-social-media-marketing-should-top-your-to-do-list/. Accessed 28 May. 2019.

traffic. It is vital that business owners understand that simply having a website is not enough to drive traffic to their business. When new content is uploaded, it can be quite difficult to raise awareness about products or services. There are likely hundreds or thousands of other websites that are selling similar products to you. As a result, you have to stand out to be ranked high on top search engines such as Bing and Google. Incorporating social media marketing is a great way around this competition. If implemented correctly, social media marketing is the most effective way to increase traffic to your online store.

Boosting Your Website SEO

In relation to what has been said about increasing your website traffic, using social platforms also improves your website SEO. SEO stands for search engine optimization. This essentially is a measurement of how high search engines will rank your content for particular search terms. Of course, every business-oriented individual posts content with the hopes of it being ranked high on search engines such as Google. However, this is often not the case, as some pages end up being ignored and ranked poorly. This is influenced by the traffic that one gets to their website. If people are not frequently accessing your website, it implies that your content is not as engaging. Search engines will make the assumption that your content is not relevant. As a result, you'll find that your business website does not appear on the first page of any search engine results.

Increasing Your Reach

"Reach" is a term used in social media marketing to refer to the number of individuals who see your content[3]. The use of social

---

[3] "Reach vs Impressions: What's the Difference in Terms? | Sprout Social." 15 Feb. 2018, https://sproutsocial.com/insights/reach-vs-impressions/. Accessed 28 May. 2019.

networks will indeed increase your reach. Instead of reaching a small population, social media platforms will boost your reach to a wide market. Without social media, it would have been near impossible to reach out to thousands of people as easily as a business can nowadays using Facebook, Instagram, Twitter, and other social networks. Most businesses track their reach to determine whether their social media marketing strategies are working out or not.

Gaining a Better Understanding of Your Audience

People use social media pages to get social. Individuals turn to these pages as a way of enhancing their communication. As a business, you shouldn't make it too obvious that you are out to promote your goods or services. Your followers need to see you interacting. Therefore, besides posting engaging content, you should strive to be part of the social community.

The advantage gained by using social media pages is that one gets to understand more about their target market. Going through their posts will say a lot about what your customers expect; you will learn about their behaviors. Therefore, from this information, you can tailor your marketing efforts to convince them that you can meet their demands. For instance, by knowing the kind of posts your audience members love to share, you can focus on sharing similar posts. This will increase your chances of getting their attention since you will only be sharing the content that they enjoy seeing on social media.

Consequently, the significance of using social media for your business goes beyond boosting traffic to your website. These platforms also allow you the opportunity to get to know your audience better.

Building Stronger Relationships with Your Audience

Most businesses fail when using social media to promote their businesses because of the hard sell approach they use. Your customers are using social networks to interact with their friends and relatives, as well as to entertain themselves. Keeping this in mind, for your marketing efforts to succeed, you should also interact with your leads. This means that you should not directly use Facebook or Twitter to sell your products. Most individuals will ignore your posts and messages simply because they don't resonate with what they are on social media platforms for in the first place.

However, if you can approach your followers authentically without trying to hard-sell them right away, they will be much more likely to follow your brand. People will follow your brand because they are under the impression that you will listen to and communicate with them. Additionally, through your engaging content, customers will feel compelled to follow you in order to gain access to the content you will share in the future.

Through the dedicated following you generate for your brand, you will find it easy to build strong relationships with your target audience. This is because you understand what your audience loves, and your posts will only feature content that will resonate with them.

Benefit from Targeted Ads

Another reason why it is important to advertise your brand on social media is because of targeted ads. There are numerous tools you can use to approach your potential clients. Some of these tools are free, whereas others are paid. With the help of these marketing tools, you can narrow down your marketing efforts to only target a few specific individuals. For example, marketing tools can be utilized to reach customers based on criteria such as their location, age, occupation, shopping behavior, hobbies, etc. This data can be obtained from the number of pages that a user has liked among other things.

If a user's social platform shows that they like pages relating to sports, then it is quite likely that they like to use sports equipment or gear. For that reason, if your business deals with sports-related equipment, you can target your followers based on these interests. This is how social media can help you narrow down your target audience to reach a small population. You should realize that this will boost your chances of turning your leads into followers, and eventually, customers.

Enhanced Customer Service

The advent of the internet has transformed the way in which customers relate with brands and businesses in general. The internet has made it possible for businesses to improve their customer service greatly. Today, there is a lot demanded from customer service with regards to response time. When customers encounter issues when using your products, they expect solutions right away. Oftentimes, they turn to social media pages to express their frustrations. Business owners should be careful not to disappoint their clients, as any failing can quickly become public online and deter potential future customers. Consequently, businesses should respond immediately and politely to customer queries. This helps to create a good image of their brand.

Building Brand Loyalty

Engaging with potential customers on social media builds brand loyalty. It also helps customers to see you as a brand that cares for them. Your business social media page should provide your customers with useful, engaging, and entertaining content. Remember, you are not asking for anything in return for the quality content you are sharing. Your followers should simply gain the perception that you value them. They should realize that you value them as people and not just as a means to increase your return on investment. When people see this in your business, they are likely to become more loyal to your brand. Ideally, you will gain a competitive edge over other businesses through increased brand loyalty.

Counter Competition from Rivals

There are millions of brands that have turned to social media as an ideal way of reaching their customers. As a result, in order for companies to combat this competition from their rivals, they also have to use these platforms. A majority of companies are indeed benefiting in some way from social media marketing. This is because promoting products and services on these pages is somewhat straightforward. However, many companies are not experiencing the full benefits available because they are not using these platforms in the most effective manner.

Businesses typically try out social media marketing quickly without taking the time to understand how it should be incorporated into their marketing strategies. A lot of these businesses don't get results as quickly as they'd like, and then fail to invest further in online marketing. Just like any other marketing strategy, using social media also requires one to invest both time and money in order to get the desired results.

Since most of your business rivals are probably already using social media to promote their products and services, you also should have an online presence to counter their competition. This goes beyond just posting content on the internet. You must master how to effectively promote your brand on social media in order to stand out. More tips will be provided later in this book to help you create engaging content that will lure customers to your business.

Learn from Competitors

The fact that most of your business rivals are on social media implies that you also need to be on these networks. This is the best way in which you can compete with them in today's market. Another huge benefit you will receive by using social media is that you will learn from your rivals. If you are new to the industry, the actions of your opponents on social networks will give you some information on what you should or shouldn't do. For instance, if they are advertising certain products over others, it likely means that you should be doing the same. You can watch your rivals and see what has worked best for them, drastically cutting your learning curve.

Generate Leads and Boost Conversions

Sharing content on social media will not only increase your number of followers, but it can also generate potential leads. Ideally, your marketing strategies will also increase your conversion rate. This is where you convert your leads into potential customers. This happens because you will be marketing your goods and services to people who have voluntarily chosen to follow you. As such, the main reason for following you is that they love your brand and the products you offer.

Generating leads on social media can be achieved in many ways. Many businesses choose to do so through the creation of contests. You can increase engagement on your page by encouraging people to enter in these contests. Additionally, leads could be generated through the idea of adding links that redirect your visitors to your business webpage. It is essential to note that this is only possible if you share informative and engaging content.

Establish Authority

Socialites will know more about your brand if you maintain an active presence on social media. Answering questions and actively participating in groups demonstrates your expertise in a particular field. When clients look for assistance with something that relates to what you offer, they will seek you out over other brands. This is how social media helps businesses establish authority within their industries.

Marketing on Social Media Is Exciting

Hosting a Facebook live event to celebrate the launch of your new product or posting entertaining videos to your YouTube page doesn't simply increase your reach. It also gives you the opportunity of interacting with your audience on a personal level. As the business owner, you get to share your joy with other people who also have an interest in what you offer. There is a fulfilling feeling gained here. The excitement that comes along with engaging with your customers will undeniably motivate you to maintain your high marketing standards. Compared to conventional forms of marketing, social media is fun!

There are many reasons why your business should be on social media. Considering the benefits that have been discussed, there is a certainty that your business will eventually grow if you embrace the significance of using social media as a marketing tool. Initially, you might have thought that social media will only increase awareness of your brand; however, as you have learned, there is much more for you to gain. Besides increasing brand awareness, you also get to build stronger relationships, increase your reach, establish authority, and learn from what your competitors are doing. Social media marketing is absolutely vital in today's market if you want to experience the continued growth of your business.

Chapter 3: Creating Your Social Media Marketing Strategy

As you can tell, businesses can easily benefit from this form of marketing. However, this leaves us questioning why most businesses still fail even after using Facebook, Twitter, Instagram, and other platforms to market their brands. One of the main reasons why most will fail is because they race to adopt this form of marketing without a strategy. This is what happens with most people who implement social media marketing. Perhaps you might have also fallen into this trap. You create a Twitter business page without first understanding why you need it. Others create pages without knowing how they will use them to market their products or services.

The first step that one should take is to understand the meaning of social media. This implies that they should work on comprehending the ins and outs of using social media to market their brand. There is a thick line that needs to be drawn between social media marketing and conventional forms of marketing.

Conversations made on social media are richer and engaging. They are not only consumer-driven, but they are also inclusive and transparent. Equally, it is vital to comprehend that conversations are not one-sided. A look at traditional advertising shows that this form of marketing is very different. Conventional forms of marketing are not as engaging, interactive, or entertaining as social media.

With the many social platforms out there, it becomes a challenge for any business to know what the best platform to communicate with their followers is. Unfortunately, it is also not easy to make time to productively participate in all these channels. This makes it vital to come up with a strategy that will guide you. An ideal strategy will assist you in answering important questions such as the following:

- Why is your business doing this?
- What does your business seek to fulfill?
- Who are you talking to on social media?
- What channels will you use to reach your target audience?
- Which groups should you create or join?

Social Media Marketing Strategy: What Is It?

To understand what a social media marketing strategy should look like, we will look at the most important factors you should mull over when creating one. These factors include:

- Social media goals
- Your target audience
- Content
- Your ideal channels
- The process used to execute your strategy

The foundation of your strategy should be composed of the five factors that are listed above. These essential pillars are connected. Therefore, for your marketing campaign to thrive, you must make sure that you pay attention to each factor.

Setting Your Social Media Marketing Goals

The first step you ought to take when creating your marketing plan is to set goals. The content you will be posting should relate to your marketing goals. Therefore, start by defining what these goals are. Your goals should be "SMART" goals; they should be "specific, measurable, achievable, relevant, and time-bound"[4]. When setting your business goals, you should always bear in mind that these goals will vary. Hence, your goals will vary from your competitor's.

An ideal way of setting your goals begins by asking yourself why you need your business to have an online presence. There are several reasons why your business should have an online presence. It could be that you wish to enhance your brand awareness, or maybe you are looking to increase traffic to your new website. Alternatively, you could be seeking to increase brand engagement. You can have more than one goal. So, you should not limit yourself on the social media goals you set for your business.

Prior to making up your mind on what your goals will be, you should carefully evaluate whether they are achievable; you must set practical goals. You should comprehend that they can be achieved either in the short term or the long term. Making this point clear frees you from stressing yourself over things that are not working out as expected.

Knowing Your Target Audience

Essentially, any form of marketing will require one to understand their target audience. Who is your ideal customer in

---

[4] "11-Step Social Media Marketing Strategy That ... - Fit Small Business." 7 Nov. 2018, https://fitsmallbusiness.com/social-media-marketing-strategy/. Accessed 28 May. 2019.

the market? Getting to know your customer will help you create more relevant content. Of course, it will take time for you to fully understand your customer tastes and preferences. Nonetheless, there are recommended strategies that you should adopt to help you better understand your customers.

The best way to learn more about your customer is by researching. You should look for psychographic and demographic data to assist you in creating a picture of the kind of individuals who are more likely to use your products or services. The process will be somewhat straightforward if your business focuses on a particular niche. For instance, if your business targets dog owners, getting insights about your customers will not be a daunting task.

Through your audience research, you should be able to classify them according to location, age, interests, gender, career, income level, etc. These factors are briefly discussed below.

Location

Knowing the physical location of your target audience is crucial. Besides knowing their home countries, you should narrow it down to their respective neighborhoods. This is because, if you are running a local business, it will be vital for you to know about the neighborhoods where your potential customers live. The main idea here is that your followers should gain the impression that you understand their roots. This is what eventually leads to conversions.

Age

What is the age bracket of the people you are hoping to target? Depending on the products or services you are offering, the age bracket will vary. You could either target young or old individuals, or both. No matter what you choose, you must specify this beforehand.

Interests

The content you generate will depend a lot on the interests of your clients. Consequently, you should research what their hobbies are. This information can be obtained by looking at what customers follow or enjoy sharing.

Gender

Some brands will be gender sensitive. As such, you also need to determine the gender of the population you are attempting to target.

Career

The career paths of your target audience will also be essential knowledge to have. Gathering the right information about your followers assures that you will create content that works with them.

Relationship Status

Assuming for example that you are in the wedding industry, you will want to know whether your followers are dating or not. Additionally, you need to find out whether you are dealing with married couples. Such details will assist you in designing content that engages them.

There are a number of factors you should mull over when researching your audience. The idea is not to be faultless, but you ought to make an educated guess about their preferences. Narrowing down your target audience will put you in a good position to reach them with your promotional messages.

Choosing Your Channels

A fundamental step in developing your marketing strategy will be to choose the right channels for your brand. There are thousands of social platforms where you can establish your social media presence. However, your selection should consider your business goals, customers, and available resources. You should not just choose Facebook because it is one of the best social networks out there; perhaps most of your followers are on Twitter and LinkedIn. Your marketing priorities should lie in the channels where your audience is the most active.

Creating Content

After deciding where you will be sharing your content, it is essential for you to determine exactly what you will be sharing. Content is the key to transforming potential leads to loyal customers. Post the right content, and you will fully enjoy your social media marketing experience. Knowing what to post is a fundamental step that every marketer should comprehend. This bears a huge impact on the success or failure of any marketing campaign.

Still, it is worth stating that content will vary from one social website to the other. What you post on Facebook will be different from what you post on Twitter. Accordingly, one should spend time to learn how content differs from one platform to the other. This guarantees that the right content is posted to the right platform for optimal results. More information regarding social media content will be discussed later on in this book.

Analyzing Your Rivals

Let's assume that you know the best content for your audience; however, you should not make hasty moves before first exploring who your rivals are. Take your time to do some thorough research about your competitor's actions. Get to know what they are doing on social media. How are they marketing their brands on social media? What are the main social platforms they are using? Looking at their marketing strategies will help you implement better marketing techniques, yourself. The main point here is to be smart. Content is king, but you also need to be creative about how you approach social media marketing.

When analyzing your competitors, you should understand that it is prudent for you to learn from them and not to simply copy their ideas. Seek inspiration, but do not be blinded to follow what they are doing. Try to stand out by learning from their mistakes. Your aim should be to improve through the competitor analysis you will be carrying out.

Promoting Content on Different Social Networks

It is quite funny that you might have the best content to share, and still fail in your marketing campaign. The way in which you share your content matters a lot. Since there are varying platforms for you to share your content, you should use each one appropriately. This will determine whether your followers take action on what you share or not.

You can post highly engaging content on YouTube, but if you fail to remind your audience to like, subscribe, and share your videos, you might get poor results. The same applies to Twitter and Facebook. If you are going to share content on Twitter, for example, ensure that you accompany it with an engaging image that will entice your visitors. The purpose of doing this is to encourage your followers to take action by either retweeting your post or sharing it widely.

Creating a Social Media Schedule

How will you be posting content to your business social media pages? It is important for you to have a plan on how you are going to do this. Posting content at the right time ascertains that you target your audience when they are active. As such, you must have a calendar which will dictate how often you post. Having a posting schedule doesn't necessarily mean that you should post daily. However, it is essential to maintain an active social media page. The importance of having a posting schedule is that it ensures you don't forget to post to all the platforms on which you have an online presence. Moreover, it helps to create a balance to how you post on all the social platforms.

Promoting Your Social Channels

After creating accounts on different social media platforms, you should get the word out that you have an online presence. This is the best way to get more people to follow you. So, how do you promote your social channels?

There are many places to advertise that you have a Facebook or Twitter page. Begin by doing this on your business website. Adding social buttons that direct your visitors to your social pages is imperative. The same can also be done to your email list; add social buttons to the people you frequently email.

Most businesses will simply make people aware of their social pages through other social networks. For instance, you should alert your Facebook followers if you have a YouTube channel or an Instagram account where they can also reach you. This gets members engaged with the varying content that you post to these respective social media accounts.

Evaluating Your Results

Your social media marketing strategy should also define how you will be evaluating your results. These results will tell you whether your marketing campaign efforts are paying off or not. If there is anything that needs to be improved in your marketing campaign, this can also be determined by regularly measuring your results. Fortunately, this is easily done with the help of performance metrics, which are provided by social media platforms.

Common metrics you will come across include likes, reach, clicks, engagement, and impressions. You cannot continue marketing your brand on social media without knowing whether you are reaching the right people or not. Equally, you should find out if your audience is finding your content engaging. All this information can be evaluated with the help of performance metrics.

Optimizing for the Best Results

Once you understand what your followers like, you can then take the step to optimize your content for the best results. When promoting your brand on YouTube, for example, you might realize that there are particular videos that are more engaging than others. You should optimize your marketing efforts by uploading more videos that are similar. This is the best way for you to get more followers coming your way.

Having a social media marketing strategy will warrant that you promote your brand in the right way. A plan will guide you through every marketing step you ought to take. Before posting anything on your social media pages, your strategy should have helped you understand who your audiences are. Moreover, you will have defined your goals before anything else. Accordingly, a strategy will keep you focused on doing the things necessary to reach those goals.

Chapter 4: Common Social Media Marketing Mistakes to Avoid

Starting any social media marketing campaign is never easy. Bearing in mind that you might be new to this field, there is a high chance that you will end up making mistakes here and there. To help you avoid the common mistakes most newbies make, this chapter will unveil some of the pitfalls you should avoid. Being aware of these common mistakes will prevent you from wasting your time and energy on marketing techniques that may not work.

Not Planning

You might have heard that failing to plan is planning to fail. Well, in social media marketing, this phrase is nothing short of the truth. By starting off your marketing campaign without any plan, you are simply setting yourself up for failure. Your plan should assist you in realizing how social media marketing can benefit your business. This plan should also be in line with your overall business goals. For instance, if your aim is to increase traffic to your business website, your plan should define for you the right strategy to utilize in order to reach this goal. New marketers often make the mistake of adopting social media marketing without comprehending its importance in the first place. So, never make the mistake of failing to thoroughly plan your social media marketing campaigns.

Going Overboard

It is not uncommon to see business-oriented individuals trying to grow their brands within the shortest period of time possible.

People strive to reach the top fast. Therefore, when one realizes that social media marketing has numerous benefits, they might want to create accounts on several social platforms. Slow down; this is not the right way of exploiting the benefits of promoting brands on social media. It is important for you to focus first on taking advantage of the little things that you know. For example if most of your customers are on Facebook, begin from there and work your way up. With time, you can open up other accounts as you seek to grow your online presence. The point here is that you have to improve your skills as you progress.

Hard Selling

Another common mistake made by most entrepreneurs is that they end up assuming that social media marketing is all about advertising products on Facebook, Twitter, or Instagram. One thing you should understand is that socialites don't want to be flooded with sales posts. In fact, this will discourage them from following your brand. Consider this form of marketing as the way conventional customers need to be welcomed to your old store. Truly, welcoming them with promotional messages will not convince them to buy from your business. Instead, it will push them away. Hard selling on social networks will drive traffic away from your brand. Ensure that you refrain from making this terrible mistake.

Failing to Socialize

Regular posting and updating your status will help you generate some engagement with your audience. However, you should realize that your followers will expect more from you. You are in a social community. As such, you should socialize by interacting with others on Facebook, Instagram, Twitter, etc. Join groups and participate in forums. Don't just have an online presence where you only send promotional messages to your audience. Keep your audience engaged by communicating with them. Provide them with value, and you will find your way into their hearts.

Missing Value in Your Content

The only way your potential clients will follow you is by finding something to look forward to in your posts. What is the value gained by your customers from following your brand? It is imperative for a business to understand that they should look at the bigger picture of their ads. This means that one should create content where they offer tips that are generally related to the products being offered. Your clients will feel empowered if you offer them such information in your posts for free. So, don't just talk about your products or services; give your customers a reason to like and share your posts, even though they might not be buying from you.

Expecting Fast Returns

Just like building a lasting relationship with your partner, building relations with your target audience will take time. Consequently, you shouldn't expect that you will attract a large following overnight. After all, the longer it takes for you to build a strong following, the better, because you will create lasting bonds. Always keep in mind that results may be slow, but eventually, you will benefit from the connections you generate.

Getting Defensive

Often, you will have heard people claim that "the customer is always right". In social media marketing, this mantra should guide you as you promote your brand on different platforms.

There are situations where you will encounter bitter customers. Some clients will raise issues and will want to make things personal. It is crucial that you to learn how to deal with such people. You should not lash out in return, because this will tarnish your business image as your responses will be out in the open for your followers to view. You ought to respond respectfully in a way that does not worsen the situation. The point here is that your good business image should be upheld.

Being Too Casual

There is often a thin line between being professional and being casual. Yes, you are posting content on social media, but it doesn't mean that you should be too casual. People depend on your posts to make relevant decisions that will impact their lives in one way or another. As such, it is vital for you to create an online personality that is friendly, but one that doesn't get too personal. Before posting anything on the web, evaluate its relevance in the lives of your audience. If there are potential issues with the images, texts, or videos you will be posting, make sure you correct them before publishing. You can end up ruining your business image with just the simple click of a button.

Failing to Measure Your Results

Another huge mistake that could cost you your marketing campaign is failing to measure how well you are performing. It is crucial that you measure how your marketing efforts are paying off. The significance of evaluating your marketing efforts is that you can then make necessary adjustments which will warrant that you improve. For instance, if certain content fails to be effective, you can adjust accordingly by trying out other content such as posting images instead of text or posting videos instead of images.

Mistakes will be unavoidable in your social media marketing campaigns. Nonetheless, you have to make sure that you are aware of the common mistakes you might end up making. Some mistakes can be costly to your business as a whole; therefore, you should be careful not to make them. For example, if you make the mistake of expecting fast results, you will only get frustrated. Moreover, failing to evaluate your results will also deter you from realizing that your marketing efforts are not in line with your business goals.

Chapter 5: How to Use Facebook to Grow Your Business

It has now been more than a decade since the inception of Facebook by Mark Zuckerberg on February 4, 2004. Facebook simply began as a networking platform for Zuckerberg and his college friends. As a matter of fact, students originally had to use a college domain email for them to register[5]. Today, Facebook has transformed the world of social media with over 2-billion active monthly users[6]. To businesses, this is an opportunity worth taking advantage of. With so many Facebook users, business owners can reach out to their customers who use Facebook at practically any time.

Understanding Facebook Marketing

Simply put, Facebook marketing is the use of Facebook to maintain close interactions with customers. Businesses exploit the advantage of freely creating their accounts and putting up company profiles that they can use to promote their brands. The idea behind marketing brands on Facebook is quite straightforward; nonetheless, the execution process is a daunting task.

As more and more businesses turn to Facebook marketing, its definition has also evolved. Facebook marketing is now demanding more than ever. It means more than just posting relevant content on this platform. Users have to constantly keep

---

[5] "53 Incredible Facebook Statistics and Facts | Brandwatch." 5 Jan. 2019, https://www.brandwatch.com/blog/facebook-statistics/. Accessed 28 May. 2019.
[6] "53 Incredible Facebook Statistics and Facts | Brandwatch."

in touch with their customers. They also have to follow other rival brands and monitor what they are doing on Facebook. Likewise, businesses have to engage with new potential customers.

One of the main reasons why Facebook is as an ideal marketing tool is because it provides a direct line of contact for businesses to link up with their customers. Nevertheless, the marketing platform also poses a huge risk to businesses that use it. One single mistake and everything goes down the drain. A mere erroneous post can cost the entire reputation of your company.

Facebook users should distinguish their personal pages from their business pages. Regardless, the Facebook business page should also have some personal touches. This will make it easier for your followers to relate with your brand, not because of what you offer, but because of the value and enjoyment it gives them.

Top Reasons to Use Facebook for Business

Before getting into the details regarding using Facebook to grow your business, you should know why it is imperative for your company to use this platform.

Facebook Is One of the Best Social Networking Sites

Studies have revealed that Facebook is the #1 social media platform with over 2-billion active users[7]. The platform is

---

[7] "Global social networks ranked by number of users 2019 - Statista." https://www.statista.com/statistics/272014/global-social-networks-ranked-by-number-of-users/. Accessed 28 May. 2019.

followed closely by YouTube. With this statistic in mind, many marketers are using the platform to their advantage. This means that if your business is not on Facebook, your competitors will likely win over more customers than you without too much of a hassle. Marketers who have utilized Facebook for years now argue that the platform is one of the most effective social channels to use[8].

Leading Share of Social Media Referrals

Another convincing reason why your business needs to be on Facebook is that the platform is way ahead of others in regards to social media referrals. This implies that the social network can be an excellent source to drive traffic to your business website. However, it should be made clear that it's ideal if it isn't the only source of traffic used by businesses. Relying on any one platform is generally not a good idea. Regardless, users should realize that the platform can be a valuable tool to generate potential leads that could later transform into loyal customers.

Learning About Your Target Customers

Having a business Facebook page also aids in learning more about your target audience through their ongoing participation. Your audience on Facebook will follow you because of your engaging content. You can also benefit in return as you collect information about their personal behavior. Facebook Insights is a tool that will assist you in gathering important information about your audience. Accordingly, you will find it easy to make

---

[8] "Top 10 Reasons Your Brand Needs To Be On Facebook - Forbes." 26 Jun. 2015, https://www.forbes.com/sites/jaysondemers/2015/06/26/top-10-reasons-your-brand-needs-to-be-on-facebook/. Accessed 28 May. 2019.

accurate predictions concerning what your customers will want in the future.

Humanizing Your Brand

Marketing your brand on social media platforms requires that you should embrace the importance of building social connections. In line with this, Facebook gives you an opportunity to link your brand to some form of personality. When your potential customers think about your brand, traits such as honesty, loyalty, dedication, and so on come to their minds. The one on one interactions that you make will unveil the human side of your company. For that reason, people will not see you as a mere business, but also as a brand with a personality.

Facebook Will Help You Build a Community

Using Facebook also gives you an opportunity to bring your clients, potential customers, and your fans together. These people can regularly interact with your business by providing you with the product or service reviews you need. This is a community that will provide you with the insight you need in order to improve your products and services.

Your Competitors Are Already Using Facebook

The best way of dealing with competition in your industry is not always by doing what rival companies are doing. Nonetheless, with regards to social media, this could be a totally different case. If your business rivals are using Facebook, there is a high chance that you will be missing out on numerous opportunities if you aren't using the social media platform too. Therefore, it is vital for you to have a Facebook business account, as it will help you stay ahead of your competitors.

Most Clients Opt to Interact with Companies on Facebook

You should be convinced to have a Facebook account for your business simply because most customers prefer to link with brands on this social network over other platforms[9]. This implies that it's in your best interest to avoid being left out.

Facebook Is a Huge Influencer in Consumer Buying Decisions

It is quite interesting to learn that many consumers turn to Facebook with the hopes of finding opinions regarding what they should buy. Bearing in mind that Facebook is ranked as the #1 influencer platform, it's ideal for a business to have an account.

Growing Your Business with Facebook

Now that you understand why having a Facebook account for your business is a good idea, you need to learn how to use it to grow your business. The following are some pointers that will help you boost your business growth by using Facebook.

---

[9] "Top 10 Reasons Your Brand Needs To Be On Facebook - Forbes." 26 Jun. 2015, https://www.forbes.com/sites/jaysondemers/2015/06/26/top-10-reasons-your-brand-needs-to-be-on-facebook/. Accessed 28 May. 2019.

Aim to Expand Your Network

Creating a Facebook page isn't enough to grow your business. You should find a way of reaching out to people. Connect with individuals who are highly likely to be interested in your products or services. Your fanbase will determine your reach. So, it is crucial that you ask for support where necessary. You should also post engaging content that will lure potential clients to follow you and share your content widely.

Initiate the Conversation

Your customers will not talk about your brand unless you initiate the conversation. Find a creative way of raising a conversation that is closely related to the products or services that you offer. As your potential clients debate about the topic, you should not miss finding a way of introducing your brand in to the conversation. Keeping in touch with your followers is the surest way to keep them thinking about what problem your product or service can solve for them.

Motivate Your Followers

Clearly, one of the main reasons you are posting content on Facebook is to get followers. Most businesses aim to expand their reach through their posts. To achieve this, you ought to encourage people to act. One way to motivate them is by offering discount coupons for the products you are selling. Create competitions that are hosted on Facebook. There are various ways to reward your followers, so get creative!

Your Clients Are Part of Your Story

Have you ever wondered why there are certain businesses that request their clients to leave honest reviews about their products or services? Well, these reviews are an integral part of building your company's brand. Customers gain the perception that they are part of your business success story. Eventually, through shares and likes, people will learn more about your business. They will acknowledge the fact your business is indeed meeting its customer demands and expectations.

Always Appreciate Your Followers

Through your marketing campaigns, you will realize that it is not easy to gain a large following. Therefore, you should celebrate your audience at every milestone that you achieve. When you hit 1,000 likes, give your followers a reason to believe that you are appreciating their presence. At first, it might seem insignificant, but it will pay off when your followers share your content widely.

Take Action

The idea behind getting a large following is not for you to boast about them. Getting the numbers will be useless if they are not buying your products. Therefore, you should encourage your followers to purchase your products and to encourage their friends to do the same.

Use Videos

Statistics show that video content shared on Facebook is the most engaging as compared to types of content[10]. This speaks volumes about the importance of using videos on Facebook. By enhancing your engagement with your followers, you will also have better chances of growing your business.

Keys to Succeed in Facebook Marketing

At times, we have to stop and question ourselves about what other successful businesses are doing to efficiently market their brands on social media. Some companies make it seem so easy. In reality, promoting products on social media platforms such as Facebook is never all that easy. On closer inspection, there are a few things that these companies do differently that makes them succeed.

Understand Your Audience

A fundamental step to take when using Facebook to market your brand is to understand who you are talking to. It is important for you to know which types of content will make your followers engage. Luckily, there is an easier way to do this with the help of the resources provided by Facebook. For instance, you can tailor your content using the Facebook Ads Manager tool. This is a tool which warrants that you target your followers and prospects based on their location, age, interests, gender, etc. So, one key strategy that will see you succeed in Facebook marketing is understanding your target audience.

---

[10] "15 Facebook stats every marketer should know for 2019 | Sprout Social." 19 Apr. 2019, https://sproutsocial.com/insights/facebook-stats-for-marketers/. Accessed 28 May. 2019.

Talk with Your Followers, Not at Them

The easiest way to discourage your followers from sharing your content is by talking too much about the products and services you are offering. Indeed, promoting your brand over the internet demands that you should feature it in most of your ads. Nonetheless, with social media, there is a twist to it. You should put a human face to your brand. Give people a reason to look at your brand from a different perspective. Keep your audience happy and engaged by sharing content that resonates with them.

Polish Your Content

One huge challenge when using Facebook to advertise brands is that your efforts might not lead to the actual sales you initially anticipated. At times, you might promote your brand on your Facebook page and end up getting zero buyers from your marketing efforts. Entrepreneurs should understand that most buyers might not directly come from their Facebook pages. To guarantee that you make the most out of the platform, you have to polish your content to be in line with what the audience wants.

It is vital that you make sure that the content is focused on the brand. Don't offer gifts without making your audience understand why you are offering such things. They should comprehend that the rewards are centered around your brand.

Post at the Right Time

You also need to try to post at the right time. Posting when your audience is asleep will only be a waste of time. It is worth noting that there are other businesses that will also be posting at similar times. Your audiences also have friends and relatives. They will be keen to follow their posts. As such, there is a lot that people need to keep up with on social media. If you post at the wrong time, you will certainly gain nothing from your marketing efforts.

So, you might be wondering when the right time to post is. Basically, the best time to post on Facebook will be determined by your audience. Their availability will influence your timing schedule. Luckily, you can get insights into your audience's availability through Facebook Insights. This tool will inform you of the times when your followers are most active.

Content Is King

We cannot stress enough the importance of sharing great content. Content is what will keep your followers coming back to your page. Ideally, people will revisit your page to see what you have been posting. This means that you have to keep them entertained. To meet their expectations, you should have a steady stream of outstanding content. You can achieve this by sharing content from other posts that might interest your followers. So, don't stress yourself out too much. If there is content that needs sharing, then share it; this is what social media is all about. Most importantly, ensure that you share your own original content, and not only the content of others.

Partner with the Right Groups

Facebook groups are something that should not miss out in your marketing toolbox. The good thing about these groups is that you will be joining a community with an established audience that is highly likely to have an interest in your product or service. Always remember to join groups that are in line with what you are selling.

Work with Influencers

A golden rule of thumb is to work with influencers. This applies to any social media platform you will be using. Influencers have established audiences that respect their opinions. With the right type of influencers, you can be sure to gain a massive following. Picture a scenario where David Beckham endorsed the sportswear you are selling. Obviously, a lot of people will agree with his recommendation. This is what working with influencers brings to your marketing campaigns, and to your brand for that matter.

There is a wide array of benefits you can gain by using Facebook for your business. However, this all depends on how well you use the platform. You should realize that most businesses are already using Facebook to promote their businesses. Why is it that a huge number of them are still failing? You should constantly test different methods of using Facebook to grow your business, and then refine your strategies until you experience the growth you desire.

Chapter 6: How to Use Twitter to Grow Your Business

If you have been using Twitter to promote your brand, it could be the case that things are not working out as expected. Perhaps the number of followers on your Twitter page has remained stagnant in spite of your marketing efforts. It could also be that you are not getting the retweets that you initially anticipated when you first started using Twitter for your business.

Well, the negative results you are getting don't necessarily mean that Twitter is a bad platform to use. Statistics show that about 67 percent of Twitter users claim they could easily buy from the businesses they follow[11]. This implies that you must polish your marketing skills so as to get the most out of Twitter.

Employ the Use of Twitter Cards

An ideal way of capturing your audience's attention is by making sure that your Tweets stand out from others. A great way to do this is by using Twitter cards. These cards give your Tweets a more professional look. You should also remember to share these posts on your business website as they will also redirect your followers to your Twitter page.

---

[11] "10 Insightful Twitter Statistics for Small Business - Small Business Sense." https://small-bizsense.com/10-insightful-twitter-statistics-for-small-business/. Accessed 29 May. 2019.

Monitor Your Brand

As you continue to promote your brand on social media, it is vital for you to monitor how your brand is performing. With the help of the search feature on Twitter, you can query to find out whether there are any brand mentions out there. If people are talking about your brand or the products and services you are offering, you can engage with them, thanks to the search tool. Consequently, you should not take any brand mentions for granted. If possible, appreciate the brand mentions. In other cases, ensure that you provide solutions to problems that have been identified by your followers.

Grow Your Network

Certainly, growing your business using Twitter will not come easy. You cannot grow your business if you have 500 followers year after year. It is necessary that you grow your audience from time to time. Growing your audience guarantees that your posts will be shared widely.

There are different ways by which you can grow your network. First, there is the straightforward approach of simply following other people. You can do this by using keywords to search for individuals who share content related to your brand. There is a good chance that they will also follow you in return.

You can also grow your network by finding the big players in the market. Sure, you are competing with them, but it doesn't mean there is nothing you can learn from their marketing strategies. Increase your network by following people who follow the big brands in the market.

Above all, you should always keep in mind that quality beats quantity. Hence, you should refine your followers and make sure they are not just following you, but also promoting your brand.

Work with Influencers

Just like Facebook, your business will gain a huge boost if you choose to work with influencers on Twitter. Engaging with influencers guarantees that you increase your chances of attracting a large following. This implies that you will also be generating more traffic to your business page. Influencers have the numbers. They have the people that you require to transform your company. The best part is that their opinions matter a lot with regards to consumer buying decisions. As such, working with them is an ideal method to get the right people to follow you and/or promote your brand.

Market Your Business

People will also follow you if they are at all aware of the existence of your social media pages. Don't just assume that your audience knows you have a Twitter account; put this information out in the open, and mention it on your business website. Those on your mailing list should also be informed about your Twitter page. Do not forget to include your Twitter handle as a part of any business information that talks about your brand. You should create awareness by advertising your business through any means possible.

Apply the Right Hashtags

There is a lot you need to comprehend about using hashtags on Twitter. Your tweets should feature the right hashtags for them to appeal to, and reach, your followers. Do not try to squeeze in as many hashtags as your tweet can handle with the hopes of getting attention. Your hashtags can increase the visibility of your content. Thus, it is crucial for you to learn how to use them properly.

Track Your Rival's Audience

The only way you can beat the competition coming your way is by knowing what your rivals are doing. What are they tweeting? Who are they following? Who is following them? With this information, you can determine the approach you should take to guarantee that you are competing on a level field. In this case, if you are new to the industry then knowing your rival's audiences will help you a lot. Additionally, from their tweets, you can learn more about the best hashtags which drive the most traffic.

As you use Twitter to grow your business, you should not disregard the idea of monitoring your rivals. They have been in the market for a long time and thus, they know the right way to promote their brands on Twitter.

Tweet Often

Tweeting can potentially get you the brand visibility that you are looking for. Nevertheless, you should not over-do this.

Don't tweet too often, or you will only annoy your followers. How are your followers reacting toward your tweets? If they are unfollowing you, then it is quite likely that you are posting too much. It could also be that your content is boring. Work toward understanding your audience in order for you to exploit the benefits of using Twitter for business purposes.

Share Others' Tweets

Getting the most out of Twitter demands that you also share what others are posting. If there is informative and engaging content that needs sharing; share it.

Analyze and Optimize

It is always essential that you know whether your marketing campaign is working or not. Therefore, you should analyze if your tweets are gaining the best response from your audience. If the results are not up to par, you should consider making adjustments. On the other hand, if your marketing tactics are getting you the results you anticipated, you should optimize. Your aim should be to constantly build and improve your engagement with your followers.

Tweet Evergreen Content

After tweeting for several months, you might find yourself repeating what you had initially posted. Most people find it to be a challenge to come up with new creative ideas concerning what their tweets should feature. This happens to be a common issue. To circumvent this challenge, you should do a great deal of research. You must be aware of what is happening around your brand at all times. Don't just tweet the news to your Twitter page. This will be boring for your audience as they get news from other sources. They might end up ignoring your posts altogether.

Tweet Multimedia Content

An ideal way of engaging with your followers is by posting multimedia content. Forget about posting only text; try to spice things up by posting images, videos, podcasts, presentations, etc. Keep in mind that when your followers find your content engaging, they will likely share it with their friends.

Use Catchy Headlines

You should always keep in mind that you only have a few seconds to convince your followers to go through your content and share it. Well, this begins by working on your headline. This is where you start to seduce your audience. So, make sure you use catchy headlines that will leave them sharing widely.

Tweet to Other Social Accounts

The main idea of using social media marketing is to ensure that all your marketing efforts pay off. For that reason, you also need to consider posting your tweets to your other social media pages. Be it Facebook, Instagram, or Pinterest, ensure that you post your tweets there from time to time. Expand your network by using traffic gained from other social media sites.

Common Mistakes to Avoid When Using Twitter for Business

There are some common mistakes that are usually made by people using Twitter to promote their brands. It is essential that you are aware of these mistakes to guarantee that you steer clear of them.

Inconsistent Hashtags

Let's be honest, the use of hashtags can be challenging. Sure, it might appear easy, but their execution is not that straightforward. People find it to be a challenge to know the best hashtags to use. There is also the issue of knowing the ideal number of hashtags to use on a daily basis.

A huge mistake you should never make when using Twitter for business is to fail to use hashtags at all. Hashtags increase your reach. Twitter users rely on hashtags to easily find tweets they might be interested in. Hence, for your target audience to find you, it is vital that you use hashtags consistently.

Adding hashtags should be done in a reasonable way. You shouldn't get too excited about the process and end up hashtagging everything you find interesting. Your audience will find this irritating, and it may lead to some people unfollowing you. Your hashtags should be specific to your line of business; don't confuse your followers.

Inconsistent Posting Schedule

Another huge blunder you should not make is having an irregular posting schedule. Keep in mind that not all your posts will be seen. Therefore, you should find an ideal time to post your content. Timing is the key to ensuring that your posts reach as much of your target market as possible. Remember to make good use of scheduling tools such as Twuffer and Hootsuite. These tools will help in automating the posting process for you. This gives you room to focus on other important aspects of your social media campaigns.

Advertising Too Much

Most individuals will follow brands not because they like the products and services they offer, but because of the entertaining and informative content they share. So, you shouldn't assume that people are following your brand simply because they fancy what you are offering. Look at the bigger picture, and post content that does not focus too much on advertising your products.

Using Twitter like Facebook

Another common mistake you might end up making is using similar marketing strategies for your Twitter and Facebook accounts. These are two distinct social media pages. As such, they need to be treated independently. For instance, Twitter will only allow you to use up to 280 characters whereas Facebook will allow the use of 5,000. This means that your messages on the two platforms should vary. Certainly, the message should not differ completely, but the point is that different marketing strategies should be adopted for each platform.

Neglecting Your Audience

Again, we will remind you of the significance of being social on social media. Though you will be using Twitter to raise awareness about your brand, you should not forget to interact with your followers. Listen to them. Reply to their comments and queries. Follow them when necessary. This is the best way for you to add a human face to your brand. Don't give your audience a reason to believe that you are just out there to sell your products.

Twitter is one of the best social networks we have today. With over 200 million Twitter users globally, you can be sure to entice customers to follow your brand on this platform[12]. Having a business account with this network will pay off eventually if you know how to use it properly. By avoiding the common mistakes that have been discussed up to this point, you will be on the right path to establishing a stellar Twitter presence.

---

[12] "• Twitter by the Numbers (2019): Stats ...."
https://www.omnicoreagency.com/twitter-statistics/. Accessed 29 May. 2019.

Chapter 7: How to Use YouTube to Grow Your Business

Over the past few decades, businesses have transformed and adopted new strategies to ensure that they remain competitive in their industries. Today, most companies have shifted their focus from using television to promote their products, to using the internet. Besides using Facebook and Twitter, a good number of them have chosen to use YouTube. Indeed, YouTube stands as one of the best social networks. Of course, businesses can also exploit the benefit of promoting their brands using this platform.

Why Use YouTube?

Starting a business is easy. However, working to make sure that it succeeds is another thing altogether. Entrepreneurs need to strive to make sure that their brand is accessible by many people. If people are aware of the products and services you offer, there is a good chance that they will purchase from your brand. YouTube is an excellent platform that will see to it that your brand or product is visible to your target market. Below is a succinct look at various reasons why you should consider using YouTube to advertise your business.

Hype Your Product

Perhaps you are looking to enter into a new market, and you are wondering what you should do in order for people to learn about your product. Using YouTube is a smart choice, because you can create a video showing the product in use. This video should also feature the benefits of using it.

Get Feedback

Additionally, YouTube will make it convenient for you to get feedback about your upcoming product, even when it isn't available yet. Create a video featuring a demo product you are yet to launch in the market. The response you get will give you a sign of whether your clients will like it or not. If there are any changes that should be made before introducing the end product, the same can be done in due time.

Solve Problems

Most brands that are already using YouTube understand its significance in terms of solving customer problems. Uploading videos featuring common problems that clients face while using products and showing how to solve them is a great customer service experience. You don't have to keep answering calls concerning your product defects. Simply upload a video, and you will solve your customers' problems easily and conveniently.

Increase Traffic to Your Website

YouTube will also allow you to increase traffic to your website. You can easily redirect your visitors to your business webpage through the links you share on your uploaded videos. Posting entertaining and informative videos will increase the likelihood of attracting a huge following.

Save Money

Of course, companies will want to market their goods and services without having to spend a lot. Using YouTube is a great way of saving money on your ads since you will be uploading videos for free. Compare this to traditional marketing techniques where one has to pay for TV or newspaper ads. If you use YouTube appropriately, you can end up saving a lot of money.

Benefit from YouTube Ads

With more than 1.5 billion monthly users on YouTube, you can rest assured that your ads will reach your audience[13]. Interestingly, if your videos get lots of views, you can also get paid for them.

Guide to Using YouTube to Grow Your Business

Before getting too excited about how YouTube could potentially grow your business, you ought to first learn how to use it properly. Below is a step by step guide on how to use YouTube for your business:

---

[13] "22 YouTube Stats That Matter to Marketers in 2019 - Hootsuite Blog." 22 Jan. 2019, https://blog.hootsuite.com/youtube-stats-marketers/. Accessed 29 May. 2019.

Optimize Your Channel

Getting more views on your YouTube page means that you also have a chance to earn more revenue from it. There are several strategies you can use to optimize your channel to get maximum views.

Create an Appealing Home Page

The first impression is key to winning over your page visitors from the get-go. This means that you should design an appealing home page. Create a homepage that defines what your business is all about. Your homepage should feature:

- Channel art
- Channel trailer
- Other featured channels
- An "about" page

Use the Right Keywords

Appropriate keywords should be used for descriptions, titles, and tags. The importance of using valuable keywords lies in the fact that they will boost your search engine rankings. When people query something related to your brand, they can more easily find you. Keywords will increase your brand visibility while at the same time helping you to get an increased number of new subscribers.

Optimize Your Videos

Apart from optimizing your channel, you also need to optimize your videos to ensure that you increase the length of time people watch them. Likewise, optimization will also help you to raise your audience retention rate. If there is a high number of people watching your videos to the end, YouTube will promote your channel. The platform will recommend your videos to individuals who are likely to be interested in the content you share. Eventually, this leads to more views.

So, how do you increase your channel viewership? Here are three simple ways to do this:

1. To keep your audience glued to your content, you should try structuring your playlists. Organize your videos in such a way that your audience will keep watching your content. This is a great way of ensuring they are not swayed to watch other related videos from your competitors.

2. Using the right thumbnails and titles will encourage people to click on your videos. Don't use just any old names to label your videos; make sure the titles are related to the content being posted. Consider this as your first chance to win over a potential audience.

3. Another effective way of increasing the number of viewers of your channel is by creating content centered around relevant keywords. A good choice of keywords will direct people to watch your videos instead of others. To know the right keywords to use, try searching for content, and you will notice the suggestions that YouTube provides. Use these suggestions as your keywords.

Copy What Works

Since you are new to the world of social media marketing, you might want to try different promotional ideas and see whether they work for you. In some cases, your new ideas will not work since customers are used to certain types of content. As such, it is imperative that you follow the trend. Take your time to watch YouTube videos featuring similar ads to those you plan to run on the platform. Take ideas from these videos and focus on what your audience will like. Learn from videos with the highest number of shares and likes. There must be a good reason why such videos are viral. Creating similar videos will increase your chances of getting views, likes, and shares.

Calls to Action

Posting videos on YouTube is a great way of increasing brand awareness. Your followers will learn more about your brand this way. Nevertheless, this is not the only social media goal you should have; you must also make conversions. You need people to like your videos and share them as well. Also, you want them to subscribe to your channel. This doesn't just happen out of the blue. People need to be reminded each time that they should take an action. Therefore, you should remind them to like, share, and subscribe to your channel when necessary. If you have other social media networks, your call to action message should remind them to follow you on Twitter or to find you on Facebook.

There are many ways of phrasing your calls to action. The main point should be to refresh your audience's memory that they should take action after watching your videos.

Make Your Audience Laugh

Designing a professional YouTube channel will indeed make you stand out. However, this doesn't mean that you should necessarily be super serious in the videos you post. You could add some humor to your content. There is a good chance that individuals will want to share your humorous clips with their friends. Thus, you could balance your content so that it includes both helpful information, as well as humor.

Mobile Friendly

Most people spend their time on mobile devices watching videos. As such, it is vital that you ensure your YouTube channel is mobile friendly. The video quality you post should be viewable on handheld devices.

Soft Sell

Videos on your channel should advertise your brand. The last thing you should do is hard sell. Don't post videos trying to persuade your visitors to purchase whatever you are selling. This will not work. Simply promote your videos in a way that doesn't appear as if you are pushing your target audience to buy from you.

Inform, Entertain, and Engage

There are three benefits that your audience should gain from watching your videos. First, they should be informed. They should be educated about how to use a particular product or simply learn something new that they didn't know already. Secondly, they should be entertained. Apart from learning something of value, they should also be entertained by your videos. Your posts should make them laugh, or think, or both. Their engagement comes from their willingness to like, share, and subscribe to your channel.

Promote Your Videos

It is also crucial that you promote your videos. Besides having a YouTube channel, you also need to embed these videos in your social media pages such as Twitter, Instagram, Facebook, and LinkedIn. The same should be implemented on your business website. Spreading your videos can also be done by asking people to share. Don't just post and assume people will share. It is never that obvious. You should market the videos just like any other product you are selling.

Measure Performance

Running a successful YouTube promotional campaign requires that you learn from your mistakes. You should seek to improve the quality of your videos. This means that you should often work on creating content that connects with your followers. This can be achieved by measuring the performance of your campaigns. Monitor the view rate, likes, and other key performance indicators.

YouTube marketing is about more than just uploading videos to your channel. Just like any other social media page, you should interact with your audience. After posting your videos, you must optimize them for the best results.

Chapter 8: How to Use Instagram to Grow Your Business

There is a common misconception that only large businesses should use social media marketing to grow their businesses. This is not true. Both small and large brands can benefit from the use of social media marketing. As a matter of fact, small brands need it the most since they are just starting out. Big players in the market such as Nike and Apple may still get many sales without using social media marketing. Nonetheless, they still use these platforms to their advantage.

Obviously, you cannot sell your products and services to individuals who don't know about you. If you have an online store, you cannot solely rely on page views to get customers for your products. This is the main reason why you should have a business Instagram account.

Clearly, if you don't have an Instagram account for your company, then you are missing out on numerous opportunities. Around 71 percent of businesses have accounts with this social media network[14]. It is never too late to start using Instagram as a marketing tool. Your aim on Instagram should be to find a way of driving growth for your company. This chapter will point out a number of techniques that you should embrace when using Instagram to promote your brand.

---

[14] "How to Start Using Instagram to Grow Your Small Business." 2 Jan. 2019, https://www.quicksprout.com/2018/12/31/how-to-start-using-instagram-to-grow-your-small-business/. Accessed 29 May. 2019.

Begin with Your Existing Customers

The mere fact that you are adopting a new marketing tool doesn't mean that you will be throwing away the current customers who already depend on your product. A good way to initiate your Instagram campaign is by marketing to your existing customers. Email them about your new marketing strategy. Inform them that they can now reach you on Instagram. You can skip the idea of starting from scratch by choosing to deal with existing clients as you work your way to the top.

Emailing your existing customers is not the only way to market your Instagram business profile. You can also pass out the message through other social media accounts where you are active, such as YouTube, Facebook, and Twitter. Likewise, you can also link to your Instagram profile on your website. The idea is to get the word out that you now have an Instagram account.

Showcase Your Products

With the few followers you have following your brand on this platform, you should be aware of the main reasons why they are following you.

People have different reasons for following certain brands. Social media user data reveals that about 73 percent of people will follow brands because they are interested in the goods and services being offered. Approximately 58 percent of them will follow these brands due to their entertaining promotions. About 42 percent gain interest due to incentives offered to them. Interestingly, 21 percent will follow brands because their friends are doing the same[15].

Bearing this in mind, it is clear that people will not just follow your brand because of the goods and services you offer. There is a wide array of people you will be dealing with on social media. Some will follow you because they want to be entertained. You should be aware of this to ensure you create content that fits your audience.

Making use of the statistics outlined above, you should introduce your products on your Instagram account. This is what most people will want to see on your business page.

Make Use of Shoppable Posts

Something unique that Instagram provides for your business is it offers you a way of selling your product directly to your audience through the shoppable posts that users can take advantage of. Shoppable posts are just ordinary posts, but they can also sell a product in various ways. One allows you to add a tag to the post that shows the name of the product and its price. An interested buyer only needs to click the link to be directed to your website.

The best thing about shoppable posts on Instagram is that you don't have to say anything about what you are selling. In the past, brands had to include some call to action text to direct their audience. However, this has changed as the posts can now stand on their own.

---

[15] "How to Start Using Instagram to Grow Your Small Business." 2 Jan. 2019, https://www.quicksprout.com/2018/12/31/how-to-start-using-instagram-to-grow-your-small-business/. Accessed 29 May. 2019.

Put Faces on Your Photos

Shoppers are more likely to be convinced to purchase a product over the internet when they see a face attached to it. This is a smart move to keep your visitors engaged. Instead of merely posting images featuring your products, consider adding some faces. This could be pictures of past customers who have bought your products.

The more people that find your posts engaging, the more likely you are to increase your conversion rate.

Work with Influencers

Working with influencers on Instagram is an ideal way of gaining new clients. Take time to identify influencers in the industry who have a huge following. While doing this, you must confirm that the influencers chosen are in line with the market niche you are dealing with. Don't use just anyone, but instead find an individual who might actually be interested in trying out the products you offer. For example, if you are selling sports gear, you should consider finding an individual in the sports field. Ultimately, with the help of influencers, you will also attract a strong following.

Generate Leads and Sales Through Ads

Posting images and videos on Instagram might be free, but it shouldn't prevent you from investing in Instagram ads. You can spend money to make money. Instagram ads work in a similar way to Facebook ads as you can utilize a similar ad manager.

This tool helps you automate the process, as you only need to specify your budget, location, and target audience.

The good news about Instagram ads is that there are several formats your ads can take including the following:

- Video ads
- Photo ads
- Collection ads
- Carousel ads
- Story ads

When page visitors show interest in your ads, they will be directed to your business page where they can shop. Therefore, call to action messages should never be left out. At the bottom of your photo ad, for example, you should remember to add a "shop now" call to action button. This is likely to increase your sales as people will often find it more convenient to shop without having to work through several steps to purchase a product.

Encourage User-Generated Content

User-generated content (UGC) can also help you grow your business in ways you never thought possible. Using UGC creates trust. For instance, encouraging people to participate in contests will motivate other people to do the same. The more people you convince to enter these contests, the more followers you will be getting. Other people will trust what socialites are saying and, therefore, will likely follow your brand as well.

Always Connect with Your Followers

An ideal way of strengthening the social relationships you create is by engaging with your followers. To do this, respond to their comments, follow them, answer their direct messages, and share some of their posts. It makes a lot of sense to connect with your followers. Of course, they will expect responses to their comments and queries. You should be ready to respond accordingly.

Offer Promotions

Instagram is an ideal social network for sharing existing promotions with your followers and prospects. If there are current discounts being offered on your products, you can alert your followers on Instagram, and this will motivate them to make a purchase.

On a final note regarding using Instagram to grow your business, remember to utilize the right metrics to measure performance. You have the option of using either free or paid analytic tools to gauge your performance on this platform. However, it is recommended that you start by using free tools. Once you know how to effectively use those, you can then proceed and try out the paid analytic tools if you would like.

Chapter 9: Social Media Content Strategy

Content is what you will be sharing to your social media pages. Whether you are using Facebook, Instagram, or Twitter, posting the right content is key. Creating content is not as difficult as you may have previously thought. Nevertheless, it is quite surprising to learn that most companies still fail in their social media marketing campaigns, because they don't understand what their audiences expect from them. Before deciding on what you should share with your followers and other potential clients, you should create a content strategy. This strategy will help you create the right content, post on the right platforms, and evaluate your performance. To help you comprehend how to create a good content strategy, this chapter will take you through a step by step process of developing a content strategy.

Significance of Taking a Strategic Approach to Content Marketing

Before diving into the details, it is essential to know the importance of taking a strategic approach to content marketing.

Better Preparation Will Get You Better Results

Having a plan of action can always help you find your way in what you are doing. Whether you want to grow your business or are aiming to lose weight, you must have a plan. A good plan should be based on in-depth research concerning your subject matter. For your content to deliver remarkable results, you must have a strategy behind it. Do your homework, and find out what your customers love to see on social media before deciding what you will post. Eventually, you will be able to consistently deliver content that is likely to lead to conversions.

Ability to Adjust

Having a strategy to guide you will also allow you to implement necessary changes as you proceed with your social media marketing plan. If the content you created fails to resonate with your followers, you can make any necessary alterations. Without a strategy, it will be challenging for you to point out specifically what your clients don't like.

Improve with Time

In relation to what has been said about your ability to adjust, you can be sure that you will enhance your social media marketing skills over time. At first, your content will most likely struggle to win over audiences. Nonetheless, given time, you will find exactly what your followers like.

Creating a Social Media Marketing Content Strategy

Now that you understand the significance of having a social media content strategy, you should learn how to create one.

Establish Social Goals

When creating a content strategy, you obviously will want for it to have a positive impact on your company. This can only be attained if the strategy you create is in line with the missions of the company. At the beginning of this manual, we described for you some of the social goals that you can implement in your marketing campaign. As a reminder, some of these goals can entail enhancing brand awareness, driving traffic to your business page, or generating new leads. Your content strategy should aim to meet the specific goals your business has set.

Choose the Right Platform

Sure, there is a huge range of social networks you could use on the internet; however, you must understand that having an account with all these networks will be a waste of your company's resources. For the best marketing results, you should choose the best platforms for your business. Your choice of an appropriate platform will be based on your audience. Consider where your followers are most active. Moreover, you can choose a platform depending on its popularity. If a social page is popular, there is a high chance that your customers also have an account there.

Research Relevant Keywords

At this point, you should have made a selection of ideal social platforms that you can use to reach your customers. Next, you ought to research relevant keywords to utilize on different social media sites. Keywords will boost your reach; there are numerous competitors you will be dealing with. Keep in mind that basically all social platforms are used globally. So, you have to narrow it down quite a lot in order to target a specific group of people who will want to use your product.

Using keywords will also help you monitor how well your brand is performing. There are many tools that can help you evaluate your social media marketing performance. You can monitor what people are saying about certain keywords, making it easy for you to track brand mentions.

Content Creation Process

The other thing you will need to think about is consistency in your content. Create a content guide that will help you maintain consistency across the social media sites you will be using. The last thing you need is to confuse your followers with contradicting messages.

Find Your Voice

Begin by finding a voice to associate with your business. This relates to the personality of your business. What sort of personality would you like your business to embody? Knowing this about your business will also help you choose the right platforms. For example, if you are going to adopt a professional tone, it would be best for you to consider using LinkedIn. For a friendlier and social tone, it may be better to use Instagram, Facebook, or Twitter.

Know Your Competition

Your social media marketing campaign will get you the results you need only if you understand who your competitors are. Most likely, you won't be able to get ahead of your competitors if you don't know what they're doing. Consequently, take time to find out more about your rivals' marketing strategies, and formulate a way of doing what they do, but better. Just make sure you don't end up exactly copying their strategies in the process.

Tell a Story

It is essential that your content engages with your audience in the right way. This means that it should tell a story about your company values, missions, and goals. Sharing ethical content will indicate to your audience that your brand places high regard on ethical values in society.

Develop a Consistent Schedule

Once you know who you will be reaching on different social platforms, you have to develop a posting schedule. This timetable will remind you when to post on each social network on which you have an account. You should realize that your audience will only be engaged when you post regularly.

Research shows that different social media pages will have varying ideal times for posting content. For instance, the best times to post on Facebook are from Wednesday to Sunday afternoon. As for Twitter, it is best to post during the weekdays in the afternoon. Instagram is slightly different; on this platform, it's ideal to post from Monday to Friday, either at 2 in the morning or 5 in the evening.

Timing may seem like a huge challenge for newbies. Fortunately, there are many scheduling tools that can do the job for you, allowing you to schedule posts to be shared while you are busy tending to other things.

Create a Community

Your social media marketing campaign should help your business develop an online community with your customers. As more and more brands turn to social media to promote their products, clients expect companies to develop lasting relationships with them. In line with this, your aim on social media should be to create stronger bonds with your followers. Eventually, you will have a loyal community who will stick to your brand no matter what happens along the way.

Track Performance

Finally, after developing a working social media content strategy, you must track its performance. The reason for doing this is to assist you in identifying whether any changes need to be made. There are several metrics that can help you monitor how well your content is doing.

Engagement

One of the most important metrics you should monitor is engagement. How many people are retweeting your content?

How many people are mentioning your brand? How many clicks are you getting? This data will help you gain some insight into how your content is faring out there.

Reach

You should also strive to find out how many new followers are coming your way. Your reach will reveal to you how many people your content is reaching.

Conversions

Obviously, the best way of knowing that your content is working is by seeing an increase in sales. If the content you post fails to promote sales, then something needs to be altered. Valuable leads should be gained through what you post. This is what will keep you ahead of your competitors.

Referrals

Another crucial metric you should use is your referral traffic. This metric should help you measure the number of people visiting your website as a result of social media referrals. More traffic coming to your website means that your social media marketing campaign is effective.

Bounce Rate

It is important to measure the number of new visits that leave your page immediately. This is what is known as the "bounce rate". Usually, there are various reasons for people leaving your website right away. An accidental click, for example, could make them close the tab immediately. However, if the traffic comes from your social media page, then it is highly likely that your website fell short of your customers' expectations.

Sure, having a great social media content strategy will help your business grow. You might not see immediate results, but over time, you will see an increase in followers on your social media page. Actively engaging with your followers will gradually grow your business, and more people will become aware of your brand. You should never overlook the importance of having a content strategy to help guide you on how to post information on social media.

Chapter 10: Understanding Social Media Monitoring and Listening

Posting great content on social platforms is obviously an integral part of social media marketing. Nonetheless, for you to bond with your followers, you must also listen to them. You should understand what their tastes and preferences are. Oftentimes, companies on social media spend too much time focusing on what they are posting, and they forget to listen to their clients. This leads to a scenario where businesses fail to post content that's relevant to their customer's needs. To avoid this, you need to understand the importance of social media listening and monitoring.

What Is Social Media Listening?

Essentially, social listening entails listening to or analyzing conversations centered around your brand and the industry in general. This means that you will not just focus on analyzing what people are saying about your brand, but you will also take time to consider what their comments are regarding how the industry is fairing. With the help of these insights, businesses can make informed marketing decisions.

Listening to your followers on social pages will help you garner a deeper understanding of why your customers are posting certain comments on their walls. Knowing more about them will let you better tailor your marketing campaigns. For instance, if customers are complaining on social media about your rival, you can exploit the opportunity by improving on what clients are complaining about.

What Is Social Media Monitoring?

Social media monitoring involves tracking messages sent to you on social media. It is important to monitor these messages on social platforms so that you can respond effectively to your customer's inquiries. The difference between monitoring and listening is that listening will help you understand your audience, while monitoring more so entails studying the context of what your followers are saying. Listening is about looking at the bigger picture of social media marketing. Through social listening, there are three core areas you will be enhancing: industry intelligence, competitive intelligence, and brand intelligence.

Industry Intelligence

Listening will not only help you gain insights into what people are saying about your brand, but it will help you understand how the industry is fairing. In the case of social media marketing, you will identify strategies that you can target towards key demographics. Also, the information you obtain will help you to create the best products to meet your customers' expectations. Studying the industry also aids entrepreneurs in finding the best influencers they could work with to enhance their marketing efforts.

Generally, you will be more apt to discuss the industry you are operating in. The best part is that with the information you will have gathered, creating tailored content will not be a huge task for you. This is because you will understand what people are looking for and, as a result, you'll be able to optimize your marketing strategies for the best possible results.

Competitive Intelligence

Putting your ears out there will also lead you to find out who your rivals are. Individuals on social media will want to compare your products with what your competitors are offering. This means that you can compare your product/service provision to that of your rivals. Consequently, such comparisons can be an opportunity for you to overtake your competitors in areas where they are weak.

Moreover, competitive intelligence can be achieved through learning the tactics of your rivals. To be ahead of the game, you should know how other people are playing. Studying the moves of other businesses will provide you with the information you need to counter their competition. For instance, if your rival has not used Instagram in their social media marketing mix, you can outperform them by winning over potential clients on this platform.

Gaining a competitive edge over rivals in the market of operation is always an achievement to strive for. However, it is not as easy as it sounds. To emerge as the best in the industry, you must study and comprehend what your opponents are doing in the market. This is where social media listening comes in. Simply listen to what people are saying on social media, and you can pinpoint major weaknesses other companies are suffering from. Filling this void is the best way of luring clients to your side.

Brand Intelligence

Social listening will keep you in the know concerning matters of your brand. As people interact with your brand on different social pages, paying attention to their comments will help you figure out the kind of perceptions customers have regarding your brand.

Similarly, through their experiences, you will determine whether your product is meeting their expectations or not. Customers leaving positive comments will signify to you that your brand is performing well. Conversely, if complaints flood your social pages, then something is wrong with your products.

The notion of brand intelligence will also guarantee that you stay ahead in terms of your campaign analysis. From the responses you get on your social networks, you can easily determine the best campaigns to generate more followers.

Social Media Monitoring Tools

Marketing gurus understand that keeping track of all their social media networks is not an easy task. For that reason, there are handy tools which can automate the process for you. The advantage gained in using these tools is that companies can make sound decisions in matters relating to their products and services. For instance, with the help of data gathered from monitoring tools, a user can determine whether their social media marketing strategy is paying off or not. These tools can guide a user to improve in areas with little effort.

Undeniably, there are loads of monitoring tools you can use on the internet. Unfortunately, not all of these tools are good. To help you narrow down the best tools that have been tried and tested, take a look below at some that are highly recommended.

Keyhole

This monitoring tool stands among the best in the market today. The tool is best used for Instagram and Twitter accounts. It will help you monitor your brand mentions by looking at hashtags, keywords, usernames, and URLs. Keyhole comes with a heat map feature that will show you the activity levels of your brand in different regions of the world.

Hootsuite

Another neat tool that can be used across different social platforms is Hootsuite. You can monitor your brand's activity on Twitter, Facebook, LinkedIn, Wordpress, Google+, etc. Moreover, if you are looking for software that will help you schedule posts, then this is the one for you. The varying unique features that are incorporated in the freemium software is what makes it very popular.

Twitter Counter

You may have guessed that this software can only be used to track your Twitter business page. This tool will help you evaluate how your customers are responding to your tweets. The tool has an array of widgets and buttons that can be linked to other social media pages, blogs, and websites. If you have several Twitter accounts, you can simultaneously monitor their performance all at once.

HowSociable

As previously mentioned, you should try to consistently monitor your rival's social media presence. HowSociable is a software program that can help you track how other businesses are performing on their social pages. You can track up to 12 social platforms. Users will have to pay for the tool if they wish to expand the number of sites they can monitor.

Digimind

With this tool, you can gauge the perceptions people have regarding particular keywords. You can determine whether they have positive, negative, or neutral impressions about the specified keywords. The same case applies to your brand. The tool lets you know what people think about your brand.

TweetReach

This is a great tool that will provide you with insights on how many people see your tweets. Basically, it measures your Twitter reach. The most exciting aspect of this software is that a user can discover their most influential followers using it. As such, targeted marketing campaigns can be created to increase your reach.

Sprout Social

If you are looking to give your engagement levels a boost, then Sprout Social might be the ideal choice for you. There is an array of analytics provided by the software. The information gained from such evaluations can increase your engagement considerably.

Mention

Another great app that you can use in your social media marketing campaign is Mention. This tool tracks mentions in over 30 languages. Therefore, you can be certain that your brand mentions in varying social media pages will not go unnoticed.

The tools discussed herein are just a few of the many that you will come across. The most important thing for any new user to remember is that they should not make rushed decisions when deciding on the best applications to use. Bearing in mind that some are free, it is a good idea to try these tools out first before purchasing anything. Once you determine that a specific software meets your needs, you can then proceed to make a purchase in order to maximize their benefits.

Factors to Consider When Choosing a Social Media Monitoring Tool

Undoubtedly, with the many social media monitoring tools to choose from, it can be a difficult task to decide which is best for you. For that reason, you should consider several factors that will help you in choosing the ideal tool. Some of these important considerations you ought to bear in mind are discussed below.

Reasonable Pricing

Many people will opt for paid versions of monitoring tools because of the perceived notion that they will offer better tracking. While this might be true, it is essential that you also choose software that is reasonably priced. The price tag should match the unique features tied to the product.

Number of Keywords

Some tools will limit the number of keywords that can be tracked. Consequently, you should find a tool that offers you an opportunity to have several keywords tracked.

Mentions

Just like with keywords, you will also need to find software with a reasonable number of mentions allowance. From time to time, you should study whether you are using your mentions fully. If there many mentions that are left untouched, you should consider settling for a smaller package plan.

Number of Platforms Supported

This is one of the most important considerations you should have in mind. The social media monitoring tool you end up choosing should be one that allows you to track several platforms. An all-in-one tool will help you focus on effectively monitoring how your brand is fairing on the different social pages where you are active.

Real Time Analysis

The best way of staying ahead of your rivals in your marketing campaign is by gaining access to real time updates. Your ideal monitoring tool should keep you updated on what is going on around your brand.

Defined Metrics

Of course, you also need a tool with several metrics to help you increase your engagement. For instance, it should clearly tell you your reach, brand sentiment, impressions, likes, bounce rate, etc. With the aid of these metrics, it will be easy for you to streamline your social media marketing campaigns.

Multi-Language Support

If you are operating on an international platform, then you will also want a tool that can track mentions in different languages. This means that you will not miss out on any international conversations that might be targeting your brand.

Mobile Support

The best software for you might be one that offers you the ability to work from any location. Hence, you should consider whether the application can be used on mobile devices. Ensure that it is compatible with different mobile operating systems such as iOS and Android. You must continuously monitor your social media marketing campaign, which isn't always possible if you have to use a computer to do so.

Competitor Analysis

Another vital requirement that any good tool should provide you with is the ability to track your competitors on social media. If you are looking to win over clients from your rivals, then it is imperative for you to know what your opponents are doing. You can then make the right moves that will see customers opting for your products or services.

The factors pointed out here should help you find ideal social media monitoring tools online. You should not just focus on the price. Take your time to find out whether the tools' functionality will drive you to meet your marketing goals.

Chapter 11: Growing Your Following on Social Media

It can be argued that learning is a process that never ends. Well, when it comes to social media marketing, this statement holds true! There are many things you need to be aware of for in order to become a successful marketer. After obtaining the right tools for your marketing campaigns, you still need to learn how to grow your following on social platforms. Gathering a huge fan base online around your brand is an ideal way for you to see your business grow.

Entrepreneurs who have succeeded in their marketing campaigns will attest to the fact that having a large following is a fundamental requirement for any company. You need to know how to attract a large audience to talk about the products and services you are offering. This chapter dives into the details regarding the best strategies you should adopt to increase your following on the different social media pages you use to promote your business.

Establish Your Goal and Objectives

You should begin by establishing your social media goals and objectives. What do you really want to achieve from your campaign? Before you start posting on Facebook, Twitter, or Instagram, you should be sure about what you are aiming to achieve. Which audience are you looking to approach with your marketing message? Do you know how the different platforms work? Without a doubt, the strategy you adopt on Facebook will vary from what you will use on Twitter. So, identifying your goals and objectives will warrant that you initiate your campaign in the best way possible.

Humanize Your Brand

People are on social media to interact. Put yourself in the shoes of your audience. Why would they visit their social media pages? It goes without saying that they will log in to their Facebook page to see how their friends are doing. The last thing they will be doing is checking how brands are competing in the industry. So, it is vital that you understand why individuals are on social media. Ensure that you also focus on this aspect in your campaigns.

Talk with your audience in a natural way without bringing your brand into the conversation. They should gain the perception that you are part of the community. Eventually, you will attract a large following since they will frequent your page out of curiosity.

Understand Your Fans' Needs

Most real life relationships that succeed are purely based on understanding. If you cannot understand your partner, there is a great chance that your union will not last. Everybody understands that this is true. Well, the same applies to the relationships you create with your prospects on social media. For people to trust and follow your brand, you should discern what they need. Do your homework and find out what your followers expect to read and see on social media. Tailoring your content to suit their needs will raise their interest. At some point, your prospects will want to know what your business offers. Thus, if your products solve a problem they are facing, they will follow you.

Add Social Icons on Your Website

When socialites come across great content, they usually want to share it with their friends. Make this easy for them by having social icons on your website. Some will be discouraged and might give up on sharing the content if it is difficult to figure out how to do so. Add social icons where they can simply tap on them and get directed to your social media pages. As people find your information engaging, they will also want to follow you, and having a Twitter, Instagram, or Facebook icon will make it easy for them to do this. Don't underestimate the importance of having these icons on your website.

Link Your Social Profile to Your Business Website

A practical way that you can also attract a huge following is by linking your social media pages to your website. Before individuals buy from you, they will want to find out more about your business. As a result, it is crucial for you to link your website to the social networks that you use.

Share with Everyone

Another secret to winning over followers is by sharing your content with as many people as you can; though, this doesn't mean you should be spammy. Nonetheless, you should not hesitate to share what will add value to your followers. The significance of sharing widely is that it creates awareness among people about your online presence. Other people might see the content you post and also share it on their social networks, helping to further grow your reach.

Create a Marketing Calendar

Keeping up with what will be required from you on your social media marketing campaigns is not an easy job. For that reason, you should create a marketing calendar to help you organize your activities. The benefit of using a calendar is that it will ensure you schedule your posts at the best times to maximize your reach.

Share Valuable Content

There is nothing that beats the power of sharing valuable content on social media. You can create value by providing your audience with informative content. Also, your clients will find what you share to be valuable if it also happens to be entertaining content. Businesses can also create value through the idea of sharing educational content. Before posting anything on social media, you must stop and consider whether your posts will have a positive impact in the lives of your followers. People love to be associated with brands that share valuable content. In fact, your audience is more likely to share this kind of content with their friends on other social networks. Therefore, you should find a way of being creative and share highly engaging content to drive traffic your way.

Optimize Your Social Platforms

You will also grow your following if you know how best to optimize your social platforms. Prior to posting content on social networks, try to find out what your target market is looking for. How are they making their queries on search engines? By using this information, you can optimize your social networks using keywords. What does this mean for your business? Ideally, this will make it easy for your audience to find you. So, do some research and test different keywords to see which are most effective at driving traffic to your social media profiles, and to your website.

Use Hashtags Frequently

As part of ensuring you meet your followers' expectations, you should begin to use hashtags more often. This is what a lot of people are using today to communicate, and to find new content to engage with. This means that for you to interact with them on the same level, you also need to use these hashtags appropriately. Hashtags are mostly used on Twitter, but this should not limit you from using them on Instagram, Facebook, and other platforms. In a real sense, these hashtags will make it easy for people to trace your business. However, don't overuse them; simply use them enough to maximize their benefits.

Add Social Buttons to Your Emails

Let's stop for a moment and think about this - if you are sending emails regularly to your clients, why don't you add social buttons to the emails you send? Clearly, if you are providing your customers with quality products, they will want to know more about your brand. Some people will want to know whether there are other services you provide. Consequently, it is always a great idea to add social buttons to your mailing list.

Give Your Audience Some Benefits

Most people will have the perception that they should get something in return by following you on Twitter or subscribing to your YouTube channel. Make it clear to them that there is something in store for them if they like, share, or subscribe. This is most likely what you've seen other businesses do on social media. Some offer discounts to the first 100 customers that shop from them, and others may offer free goodies to clients who are loyal to their brands. You ought to find a creative way of raising the interest of your prospects. At first, this might cost you, but in the end, your marketing efforts will pay off!

Branch Out

You want more people to follow you, so it is vital for you to think beyond having a Facebook page. There are other prospects who have accounts on Twitter, Instagram, YouTube, LinkedIn, and more, so you should establish your presence in two or more social networks. Keep in mind that you don't need to have an account on all social media platforms, as mentioned earlier. However, be certain you have an account with the social pages where you think your audiences are most pervasive.

Use Games

If you have been using Facebook as your primary social network, you might have noticed the many games that they offer to their users. Why do you think these games are offered? Simply put, they are a way of keeping people engaged. Facebook users are likely to share their trivia game results for their friends to try. With this idea in mind, you could also make use of games in your marketing campaigns. Get people to play games, as this will spur interest and drive traffic to your business page.

Ask Your Clients to Follow You, Share, and Connect

Don't just assume that people will follow you because you offer good products or because you share great content. Some will enjoy your posts but they might not follow you or share your content. As such, it is imperative to take it upon yourself and ask your clients to follow you. Ask them to share your content on their social media pages. This is a great way of gaining attention from those who need to be reminded to take action.

The strategies of increasing your social media following discussed herein is not a complete list of what you should be doing, because the platforms are constantly evolving. You must embrace the idea of learning from the best. Use your monitoring tools, and study what your competitors are doing to drive traffic to their social media pages. You may be surprised to learn that they are doing what you do, but in a more efficient way. Or, you might even discover some new tactic that is working well for them, that you could implement yourself. So, monitor the market and be ready to employ a variety of strategies to grow your following and ultimately grow your business.

Chapter 12: Running Ads on Social Media

Any campaign you create to advertise your company will require you to pay for advertising. This is what most companies do to reach their audiences. With conventional marketing to increase your sales leads, it is normal to create several ads for TV, radio, and even within magazines and newspapers. The idea is to get the message out to as many people as you can. Just like with traditional marketing, marketing your business on social media also requires you to run ads. This chapter will take you through the process of doing this on the different social media platforms. From the information provided, you will be in a better place to get the most out of your ads.

Types of Social Media Adverts

Before going into detail about the forms of social media ads, you should settle for the social networks that best suit your business needs. In this case, you ought to mull over your social goals before choosing any platform. For example, if you are looking to reach more women on social media, it would be wise to use Pinterest as your ideal social network. This is because Pinterest is used by more women than men[16]. Conversely, if you are looking to take a general marketing approach, using Facebook or Instagram as your ideal channel would be a good move.

---

[16] "10 Pinterest statistics marketers must know in 2019 | Sprout Social." 21 May. 2019, https://sproutsocial.com/insights/pinterest-statistics/. Accessed 30 May. 2019.

It is important to understand that your choice of platform to run ads on will have an impact on these advertisements. Using the wrong platform, for example, will result in your ads not being as effective. So, before determining that your ads are not up to par, consider that you may be posting your ads on the wrong social networks.

Facebook Ads

When running Facebook ads, there are three major objectives you will be aiming to achieve. First, you will want to raise awareness about the existence of your brand. This is the same thing as increasing your reach. You will want most prospects on social media to know that your brand exists. Secondly, your goal will be to get your audience to consider what you offer. This means that you want to generate traffic, generate leads, and enhance engagement. Third, from the ads you will be running on Facebook, you want people to buy from you. Hence, you anticipate making sales conversions out of those leads.

Photo Ads

To ensure you meet your goals, you should run photo ads. Don't just use text. You can increase your engagement with your audience by using photos. Photo ads are best used when introducing a new product or service to your followers. The photos you choose should not simply feature the product itself but should also show people using the product. This will make your photo ads more convincing.

Video Ads

You also have the freedom to post video ads on your Facebook page. Facebook gives you the liberty to post either long or short videos. This means that you should comprehend how your followers use their Facebook pages. If most of them don't watch long videos, you should refrain from posting long videos. Also, you should consider the devices they use to access this network. Since most of them use their mobile devices, it would be wise to post short videos. These videos are more engaging as compared to long videos. What's more, they also have a higher completion rate. You might also choose to add subtitles to your Facebook videos, as a lot of people watch the videos on Facebook without sound.

Story Ads

Story ads are also a great way of connecting with your audience. These ads feature selected pictures that can be used to tell a story. It is important to note that these ads will only last for 24 hours; therefore, you must maximize the limited time by featuring the most important products or services your brand is offering. Don't create complicated ads for them, as you will only discourage your audience from being interested in what you offer. Remember to add a call to action button at the bottom of these stories.

Carousel Ads

Just like story ads, carousel ads will allow you to bring several pictures or videos with separate links together on each piece of content featured. These ads are ideal to showcase the varying aspects of a product that a customer should be aware of.

Equally, if you have multiple products to show your clients, using carousel ads works like magic. Your visitors will only need to watch a single ad that includes everything.

Slideshow Ads

This form of ad also features a collection of static images. One good thing about these ads is that they are easy to create. Consequently, you don't need any form of expertise to create good slideshows.

Messenger Ads

No stone should be left unturned when marketing your business on social media. Facebook makes it easy for you to interact with your audience through the Messenger app. Therefore, you should make good use of it by posting ads encouraging your audience to connect with you on the app.

Instagram Ads

If you have been following the news, then you probably know that Facebook owns Instagram. Facebook acquired the social media network in 2012[17]. Due to its ties, it is not shocking that posting Instagram ads will also support your social media objectives, such as creating awareness and increasing your conversions. The mere fact that Instagram stands as one of the most popular social media platforms should make it clear that

---

[17] "What Company Owns Instagram? Five Companies ... - Newsweek." 26 Mar. 2018, https://www.newsweek.com/facebook-own-instagram-does-companies-apps-data-860732. Accessed 30 May. 2019.

you can benefit from posting your ads here.

There are different types of ads you can post on Instagram, which are outlined below.

Photo and Video Ads

When posting photo and video advertisements, you'll notice that your posts appear in a similar manner to your normal posts. However, if you look closely, you will see that there is the term "sponsored" attached to these posts. Contingent on the ad campaign you will be running, you have the freedom of adding a call to action button to your post.

An important thing to recall when posting your ads on Instagram is that they should remain consistent. If you are using a particular theme, ensure that it is consistent throughout your ads. This will prevent your audience from getting confused.

Carousel Ads

These ads are similar to the carousel ads that you can post on your Facebook page. It's vital to keep in mind that the images should be related. Also, your followers should find it easy to swipe.

Collection Ads

Collection ads are also similar to Facebook ads. Make sure you maintain consistency as you post these ads on your Instagram page, and don't forget to feature your products and services on them.

Instagram Story Ads

It is never a bad idea to incorporate Instagram story ads to your marketing kit. After all, this is what entices your audience to keep sharing your content. For optimal results, you could spice things up by adding interactive elements.

Twitter Ads

There are several business objectives that Twitter ads will help you attain. Ads on Twitter can assist you in increasing the engagement level with your customers. Posting ads will help initiate conversations focused around your brand. Equally, the ads will increase your following. You will be charged for each click you get from Twitter referrals. Obviously, the more followers you get, the more awareness you will create about your brand and the products you offer.

Unlike Facebook and Instagram, there are a few ways by which you can create ads on Twitter. You can either use Twitter Promote or Twitter Ads (or both), to create ads on the platform.

Twitter Promote

Twitter Promote relies on the Twitter algorithm to advertise your tweets to a specified target audience. When posting ads using Twitter Promote, you can be certain that it will help you garner new followers.

Twitter Ads

Campaigns through Twitter Ads will tailor your advertisements to suit your business goals. For remarkable conversion rates when using these ads, you should post different ones for desktop and mobile users.

YouTube Ads

Over the past few years, there has been an increase in the use of YouTube to promote brands. This is influenced by the increased popularity of watching videos online. Videos are much more engaging as compared to text and images. While using YouTube to advertise your brand, you will be meeting a number of business goals, with one being collecting leads. Also, bearing in mind that your audience will be curious to know more about your business, it means that you will likely drive traffic to your website. Certainly, your brand will be recognized through your ads on YouTube and, as a result, you will also benefit from an extended reach.

TrueView Ads

These are the usual ads that play before you watch a video on YouTube. The ads can also be shown after other videos have played. Often, users have the freedom to skip videos after five seconds. YouTube recommends that these ads be 30 seconds in length or less. Nevertheless, if your content is compelling, you can create longer visuals.

Most people wish to skip these ads quickly. Accordingly, you should exploit the small window of opportunity you have to convince your audience. If there is a vital message that you must deliver, always ensure that you mention it within the un-skippable time frame.

Non-Skippable YouTube Ads

There are those YouTube ads that users cannot skip. Often, these ads appear in the middle of other videos. If you have faced this interruption when watching videos on YouTube, then you understand how frustrating these ads can be at times.

The mere fact that these ads cannot be skipped doesn't necessarily mean that your visitors will watch them. A tip that you should always have in mind is that your ads should be very compelling. Your audience will most likely do something else as they wait for the ad to run, so the audio should be captivating.

Bumper Ads

These ads run right after a particular video comes to an end. The trick to maximize the benefits from these ads is to begin on a high note. Capture your audience's attention from the get-go. Also, before the ads come to an end, ensure you use effective calls to action.

Social Media Marketing Tips

Knowing how and where to market your brand on social media does not automatically guarantee that your marketing campaign will thrive. Social media has existed for years now, and companies are still struggling to gain a strong social media presence. This proves the fact that promoting brands on social networks is not easy. To help you sail smoothly, some of the top marketing tips to bear in mind are detailed below.

Work with a Plan

It is always wise to have a plan to guide you in your social media marketing campaigns. This plan should first define your goals. Before creating accounts on social media networks, you first need to determine what you aim to achieve. Knowing what you want warrants that you tailor your ads to meet these goals.

Having a plan will also push you to conduct an audit on the different social media networks you have at your disposal. This means that you should research the platforms where your audience is most active. Moreover, your audit will unveil how your social media presence contrasts with that of your rivals.

Evidently, the idea of working with a plan also implies that you ought to have a calendar to guide you on how to post content to social pages. From what we have discussed in this book, there are varying times you should post to make sure you reach your followers.

Use the Right Platforms

Once you have defined your goals, you must cross-check this with the platforms you wish to use. The social networks you will use should drive you to meet your goals. For instance, if your aim is to reach young people, you might want to avoid using LinkedIn. It is vital that you choose the right platform, as it will increase the chances of your marketing campaign succeeding.

Know Your Target Group

Knowing your target audience is another fundamental thing that you should do. Certainly, you cannot create effective ads if you don't know anything about the people you are targeting. Do your research to understand the age, gender, location, income levels, and other factors that are essential to your business.

Use Multimedia

To get the most out of your ads, you also need to focus on using multimedia. People on social media seek entertainment. Most of them will quickly press play without reading text. This is why multimedia is more engaging compared to text. Of course, this doesn't mean that you should avoid text completely; simply create a good blend of text and multimedia. Most importantly, be creative and post good content.

Quality over Quantity

A novice marketer will want to have an online presence on almost all social media networks they can think of. The main reason for doing this is the perception that an increased social media presence will lead to many followers. However, it is crucial for any marketer to consider quality over quantity. Most successful businesses have made it big on social media while having accounts with less than five networks. The idea is to understand your target audience and focus on the few networks where they are primarily found. Additionally, by creating value on the few social pages you do have, you can rest assured that you will attract a large following. So, it is not about having ten different social networks, but rather creating value for your audience.

Use the Right Tools

There are many tools that can help you with your social media marketing. There is a good reason why these tools are freely available on Facebook, Instagram, and YouTube. They can help you save time and money that you would have otherwise used to track the performance of your campaigns. Before rushing to use any tool that you find online, ensure that you read through reviews to determine if it meets your marketing needs.

Engage with Your Target Audience

In order to succeed in your social media marketing campaigns, you should not forget the main purpose of social networks. People are on social media to interact. For that reason, your ads will only thrive if you keep your followers engaged. Track mentions on your social networks and listen to what individuals are saying about your brand. Respond to their questions and participate in discussions. Don't just run ads and expect a following to come.

Test Your Ads

The exciting aspect of social media is the immediate feedback one gets. After posting your ads, you should gauge their effectiveness. Find out whether you are getting more views on YouTube. Use your ads to determine whether you are getting more likes on your Instagram or Facebook. Based on the feedback you get, you can optimize for the best performance. It is always wise to keep refining your marketing strategy until you are satisfied with the results you are getting.

Get Inspiration from Successful Brands

As a newbie at using social media to promote your brand, you should never hesitate to learn from what the best companies in the industry are doing. In fact, you have the freedom of adopting some of the marketing techniques they are using to garner a huge following. You ought to be inspired by their actions and adjust your strategies accordingly.

Chapter 13: Tips and Tricks to Improve Your Social Media Conversion Rate

By now, you should have some idea of how to create engaging content that will resonate with your audience. Also, you should be well informed about the best strategies to utilize when posting ads on social networks. Obviously, you should also expect visitors to watch your ads. The importance of posting ads on social media is not for your audience to simply watch. In accordance with your social media marketing goals, you should also convert your followers into loyal clients. It is crucial that you increase your conversion rate as this will have a huge impact on growing your business. So, how do you go about this?

A Little Research Will Help

Let's begin with the nitty-gritty; the first thing you should do is find out who your followers are. What do they like to do? What are some of their interests? How old are they? Which areas do they live in?

This tactic is vital for a number of reasons. First, by understanding who your followers are, you will be better able to personalize your messages. This infers that you can create stronger bonds with them since you know them on a personal level. Equally, if you never had any idea of who your prospects were, you can now begin to create a picture of who they are. So, it is imperative that you first take the time to dig for more information about your followers.

Initiate Personalized Contact

Another thing you ought to bear in mind is that your clients yearn for attention. Who doesn't love being treated in a special way? We all do, right? Therefore, you should find a creative way of sending personalized messages to your audience. When sending out these messages, you must make them specific. The person receiving your message should be impressed that you know a lot about them.

When initiating personalized contact, remember not to sound too pushy with your calls to action. Think of it as your first date with your client. Undeniably, if you appear too much like you're trying to make a sale, you will ruin things. One step at a time, give your followers an opportunity to be curious about your business.

Embrace the Art of Giving

You have likely heard the phrase "what you give is what you get". Well, not surprisingly, it applies to your social media campaigns. Continually give your audience great content, and you will over time gain a large and loyal following. If you want your followers to become your loyal clients, you must master the art of giving. Since you understand their needs, don't hesitate to meet them by promoting your brand. Continue sharing good content, and you will see an increase in your conversion rate.

Find a Balance

Undoubtedly, it can be overwhelming to market your brand on social media, as there is a lot that you could and should do. A new marketer might be confused along the way. Don't just promote, but also ask questions, provide unique content, personalize your posts, and engage your audience. Yes, there are several social media activities that you should tend to, which can at first seem quite overwhelming. Be patient, and work on finding a balance between your different marketing activities.

Why is it important to find a balance? Simply stated, balancing your marketing activities will ensure your followers don't get bored. If you keep posting the same content, they will get bored eventually, and engagement will drop.

Loyalty Begins with You

It shouldn't come as a surprise that you must be loyal for your followers to return the favor. To prove to your audience that you are loyal, you should be consistent in how you post. Your audience should know when to anticipate your messages. Therefore, use a schedule in order to remind you of the best times to post.

Additionally, you can also show your loyalty by respecting the connection you share with your target audience. If you are going on a vacation, be clear about this. Inform your followers that you will not be posting for a week. This gives them the impression that you treasure their time.

Be Exclusive

Socialites fancy the idea of getting something in return. Therefore, you should offer your target audience special rewards for shopping with you. This is what will transform them into loyal customers.

Encourage Current Customers to Share

Another trick you should use is to encourage your current customers to share your content on their social media pages. This is important, because most people trust their friends. It can be very difficult for an individual to trust a strange brand promoting its products or services. However, recommendations from their friends will be highly considered. Along with transforming your followers into loyal customers, you will also grow your business.

Promote Your Followers

It is essential that you also return the favor by promoting the followers who have a huge impact on the success of your brand. Schedule appropriate intervals to do this without doing it so often that it becomes irritating. Use this opportunity to make these individuals feel special. Others will gain the perception that you really care about your followers. This is a good way of building your image. Over time, your audience will value your social media presence more and more, and will grow loyal to your brand.

Testimonials Work Like Magic

People will not fail to appreciate the value they get from your business. As such, you ought to provide them with the opportunity of expressing their appreciation on your social platform. Ensure that this is made visible to your followers. Testimonials from other clients will help you build trust among your audience. Moreover, the positive comments you get will be a constant reminder to your prospects that your products and services are high quality. This will lead to a higher likelihood of other people being motivated to try what you offer.

Make Yourself Reachable

When you use ads to post links directing your audience to your website, you should confirm that these links are working. If your followers fail to find what they were expecting, they might not click any links from you again. Give your audience an easy way of reaching you by using social buttons on your business website and other social media accounts. Your target audience needs to find it easy to share your content, so help them out.

Making use of the pointers discussed throughout this chapter will see your business grow through the increased conversion rate you will be experiencing. From the information provided, you should understand that getting more from social media campaigns requires more than just posting great content. People need to be reminded to take action. They also need to see you engage with your followers. Reward their efforts by giving them praise and promoting them on your social media page. Remember to pay attention to their needs as this is the only way they will realize that you are a brand that cares about them.

Chapter 14: Motivation from Businesses That Made It on Social Media

To most new business owners, seeing is believing. Running a successful business can become easier thanks to the inspiration that you get from those who have succeeded before you. Indeed, this also applies to real life experiences. For people to remain focused on their goals, it often helps for them to seek motivation from other individuals. Today, there are numerous businesses with success stories due to the use of social media to promote their brands. Some of these companies will be discussed succinctly in this chapter. Knowing that there are other brands out there that grew their businesses through the use of social media should motivate you to maintain a positive outlook with regards to social media marketing.

Dacia

Dacia is a car brand company that is mostly known for being Renault's subsidiary[18]. Using Facebook as their main social media marketing platform, the company has grown tremendously over the past few years. Their social media marketing goal was to create brand awareness and to increase sales leads, and their main focus was to deliver targeted ads to be viewed by both mobile and desktop users.

The results they obtained from their marketing campaigns made a huge difference to their business. First, with regards to

---

[18] "5 Successful Social Media Campaigns You Can Learn From | DMI."
https://digitalmarketinginstitute.com/blog/5-successful-social-media-campaigns-you-can-learn-from. Accessed 31 May. 2019.

their advertising costs, they saw a drop in costs by 45 percent. Equally, they experienced a 27-point enhancement in their ad recall rate.

Following the positive results gained by Dacia, a lot can be said about using Facebook to generate leads. When utilized correctly, the platform can provide an extremely cost-effective means of promoting your brand.

Tvibes

Tvibes is yet another successful company using the Facebook platform to drive traffic and attract a huge following. The organization gives its users the opportunity of creating their own TV channels just by using their smartphones. Since their inception in 2014, they have risen to become a leading brand on social media[19]. Their main goal on social media has been to establish loyalty, while at the same time engaging users to take advantage of their app.

Following the use of social media, the company saw a rise of new app installations by 50 percent. Take note of the fact that this was driven by Facebook. Their engagement rate also went up by 20 percent[20].

Due to their positive results, one can deduce that clients who are gained via Facebook are likely to become loyal to a particular brand. The use of video ads is also an effective way of creating engaging campaigns.

---

[19] "5 Successful Social Media Campaigns You Can Learn From | DMI." https://digitalmarketinginstitute.com/blog/5-successful-social-media-campaigns-you-can-learn-from. Accessed 31 May. 2019.
[20] "5 Successful Social Media Campaigns You Can Learn From | DMI."

Red Bull

This is not a new one, right? Well, the company has been gifting people with wings for more than 20 years now. In spite of the brand's already wide recognition on the international scene, it exploits the use of social media to promote its new products. It uses Instagram with the goal of raising awareness about the new flavors of products released to the market.

Due to its optimized campaigns, Red Bull reached 1.2 million customers. It also saw its brand increase in favorability by 9 points. In terms of awareness, they reached a 10 point increase[21].

What can you learn from this brand's use of social media to market its products? Honestly, it doesn't matter whether you have a big or small company; social media marketing can still have a profound impact on your business when used correctly.

Slack

Another company that has recently hit the headlines is Slack. During its inception in 2014, it had only 15,000 users. Six months later, the platform had over 171,000 users. One year after it launched, it boasted over 500,000 users[22]. You must be wondering what their secret is. Their trick is offering customers a unique experience. Their high response rate on social media has greatly contributed to an increased following on Twitter.

---

[21] "5 Successful Social Media Campaigns You Can Learn From | DMI." https://digitalmarketinginstitute.com/blog/5-successful-social-media-campaigns-you-can-learn-from. Accessed 31 May. 2019.

[22] "11 Companies That Are Killing It with Their Digital Marketing Campaigns." https://www.convinceandconvert.com/digital-marketing/killing-it-with-digital-marketing-campaigns/. Accessed 31 May. 2019.

The lesson learned from this company is that a business should aim to provide a solution to the challenges that users are experiencing. It is not just about the product you are offering; people are more concerned about the problem you are solving. So, does your product offer a solution? This is what has been discussed in other sections of this manual. Your social media campaign should not just focus on your product. Give your followers a reason to follow you. The value that they gain by following you is what will see your business grow exponentially.

JetBlue

This is another good example of a company that sets the right tone for how social media platforms should be used. A huge mistake that most businesses make is focusing their ads solely on themselves. Oftentimes, these companies fail because no one follows them. JetBlue makes excellent use of Twitter to offer an exceptional customer service experience. Surprisingly, the airline company rarely uses the platform to post about the huge discounts that it offers to its esteemed clients. Instead, most posts are responses to help its audience get the best service.

Today, the brand has close to 2 million followers. An important lesson learned from this company is that social media marketers should try to create value through their marketing campaigns. Also, a high response rate on social media will eventually pay off.

Domino's

Domino's is another company that has really transformed through the use of social media as a marketing platform. The pizza company came up with a creative way of ensuring that their clients didn't have to struggle to get their pizza. Domino's initiated the "#EasyOrder" hashtag on Twitter in May 2015[23]. Customers could have their pizzas delivered by simply using the hashtag. Following the success of this marketing strategy, the company gained immense recognition from the likes of Forbes, Good Morning America, and USA Today. Amazingly, they also won the Titanium Grand Prix prize. This is how social media can put your business in the limelight. You only need to be creative about how you use it.

Airbnb

Airbnb attributes its success to the influencers they used on social media to drive traffic to their website. The company exploited the advantage of working with notable individuals in the entertainment industry. These people helped the brand grow within a short period. Some of the celebrities that they used includes the likes of Lady Gaga and Mariah Carey[24]. With over 2 million people now using their platform, this speaks volumes about how social media marketing can have a huge impact on the success of your business.

It is worth noting that Airbnb uses Instagram, Facebook, and Twitter as its main digital marketing platforms. Their content is highly engaging since it features user-generated content. The images and videos they share on their social networks spur interest in the minds of their audiences. This is what contributes to the large following that they are proud of.

---

[23] "10 top social media marketing success stories | CIO." 28 Apr. 2016, https://www.cio.com/article/3062615/10-top-social-media-marketing-success-stories.html. Accessed 31 May. 2019.

[24] "Big Brands That Get Social Media Right - Business News Daily." 30 Apr. 2018, https://www.businessnewsdaily.com/10720-lessons-for-small-business-social-media-brands.html. Accessed 31 May. 2019.

Clearly, social media can indeed transform your business, though only when it is used in the correct way. The businesses that have been discussed turned to social media and exploited its use by connecting their brands with clients. Lessons learned from their digital marketing use is that companies should look beyond the products and services they are offering, and they should focus on the solution they are providing as this is what people are more concerned about. More importantly, the key to a successful social media marketing campaign is knowing what your followers want.

Chapter 15: The Future of Social Media Marketing - Trends to Follow

The digital marketing landscape is changing rapidly, and organizations need to adjust accordingly. With this quickly changing business environment, entrepreneurs need to review the future of social media marketing to guarantee its sustainability. Knowing the future trends of social media can also help your company to optimize and get the best results. This chapter will take a look at some of the most important social media trends that are likely to impact your campaign.

The Value of Engagement

Engagement is a crucial aspect of social media marketing. However, it is worth pointing out that most platforms do not put enough stress on sharing meaningful content. For instance, Facebook will demand this from your social media marketing activity. Its algorithm is tailored to favor content that has a high level of engagement. Therefore, if you suddenly realized that your Facebook posts have not been generating results, you should revise your engagement strategies.

Increasing your engagement levels shouldn't be that challenging if you know what your clients want. This could also be improved by sharing appealing content. Find out what your audience likes when they are using Facebook, YouTube, Instagram, and other social networks. Focus on optimizing your marketing strategy to suit their tastes and preferences. This is the best way in which a social media platform like Facebook will rank or prioritize your ads.

The future of social media marketing also requires that you steer away from the idea of using baiting techniques. Stick to genuine content for the Facebook algorithm to work in your favor.

The Growth of Groups

If you have been using Facebook for business or for personal use, then you have most likely seen the groups feature. There are major changes that the groups feature has gone through. Now, there are story updates, live videos, participation, and other features for businesses to take advantage of. The changing Facebook algorithm implies that it's ideal for companies to use groups to reach their audience.

On Instagram, there have been a few changes that you should also be aware of. For instance, the Instagram Stories feature has incorporated a new "Close Friends" attribute. By using this feature, brands can now showcase their products to a selected group of people. This tool can be helpful when introducing new products to the market, and you want to get an insider look before fully launching.

Influencer Marketing

A lot has been said about the significance of influencer marketing. Nevertheless, you should be informed about the recent changes that social media platforms have been adopting. With the increased use of influencer marketing, brands have found it difficult to stick to big names in their industries. Influencers with a massive following are quite costly for most upcoming businesses to afford. Therefore, this contributes to the introduction of micro-influencers.

Micro-influencers have a smaller following, but they can still help any business increase their engagement rates. The best part is that they are not as costly as other influencers. This means that businesses can cut some of their marketing expenses by turning to micro-influencers.

Transparency

Considering the numerous cases of privacy issues that have revolved around social media over the past decade, brands are expected to be transparent. How do you bring transparency to your brand? When users find issues with your products, you are expected to apologize on social platforms and find a way of correcting your mistakes. If possible, you should offer replacement products to those who have been affected. Honest responses about your brand are expected at all times. Also, if there are any product changes that have recently been made, you must inform your followers about this.

Social media is a great way to keep your audience aware of any changes made to your products or services.

Driving Sales Using Social Media

Social media marketing has brands not only using social platforms to increase their engagement; they are also using Facebook, Instagram, Twitter, and the likes to drive more sales. This is facilitated with the introduction of numerous tools that can help boost sales. Facebook is at the front line of ensuring that companies can increase sales by simply using social media.

To ensure that you exploit this opportunity, you should embrace the idea of using paid promotions. These ads can directly feature your products so as to increase the number of sales you will be making.

Introduction of Chatbots

As more and more people are reaching out to brands on social media, many companies are finding it difficult to keep up. There are times when you might not be available to respond to your customer's queries right away. In such instances, chatbots come in handy. They will help you meet your goal of responding promptly to your clients. Ultimately, this will have a positive impact on your business.

Basically, chatbots use Artificial Intelligence. They might not give perfect responses to your clients' issues, but they will help in rectifying the situation. Therefore, messages can be tailored to help in solving common issues that people are facing when using your products.

Stories

If you have not been using stories in your social media campaign, then you should re-strategize your content marketing techniques. At first, this was a feature provided by Snapchat. Due to its effectiveness, Instagram, Facebook, and WhatsApp didn't waste any time before adopting it. The stories feature often lasts for only 24 hours before disappearing.

Its short lifespan gives businesses an opportunity to create diverse content. The interactive nature of stories is what makes them highly engaging. Hence, companies should exploit this feature to promote their products and services. The interesting aspect of stories is that they are simple to create. Also, social media users find them captivating, because they are short.

The trend of using stories on social media is not ending anytime soon. Recently, LinkedIn also introduced the feature. This speaks volumes about the impact of this feature on social media marketing.

Live Videos

Another notable trend to watch on social media is live videos. People used live videos for the first time through YouTube in 2008. Thereafter, Facebook also adopted the feature in 2016[25]. Instagram now also offers this feature on their platform. There are numerous benefits that businesses can gain by using live videos to advertise their products. For instance, videos can be helpful when introducing new products to your audience.

Entrepreneurs can also use the feature to demonstrate their products in action. This makes it easy for people to learn how to use your product in the right way. Technical issues can also be featured as a way of providing clients with immediate solutions to the problems they are facing.

You must understand that live videos give you the advantage of interacting in real-time with your followers. Thus, this feature on social media networks will likely lead to increased

---

[25] "The Future of Social Media Marketing – 11 Trends ... - Shane Barker." 16 Apr. 2019, https://shanebarker.com/blog/future-of-social-media-marketing/. Accessed 31 May. 2019.

engagement.

Significance of Messaging

A keen eye on social media platforms reveals the fact that most of them are trying to adopt new messaging applications. This is a move that has been adopted by Facebook and other social networks such as WhatsApp and WeChat. The introduction of these messaging apps has been influenced by the notion that people want to interact in more ways than just seeing and commenting on posts. Therefore, brands also need to adopt this in their marketing mix. They need to communicate with their followers on these apps to maintain their brand visibility. Some companies have already taken up the challenge and are interacting with their customers on WhatsApp. This is a great way to reach out to esteemed clients on a personal level.

Following the discussion on the future of social media, it is important for any business to understand the direction that social media marketing will likely take. This helps them stay ahead of the game. For instance, with the recent introduction of stories, companies that were quick to use this feature to market their brands benefited. Being informed of future social media trends guarantees that you can fully exploit the benefits of advertising on these platforms.

It should come to your attention that, if you are not taking these social trends seriously, other businesses are. Your competitors will take advantage of any new marketing opportunity that social media provides them. Accordingly, to remain competitive in your industry, you also need to make wise moves and embrace these changes.

Chapter 16: Social Media Marketing - Why Most Businesses Fail

The internet is filled with all sorts of information as to how social media marketing should be conducted. Besides reading books, people can watch videos, read blogs, and gather information from other sources on the internet about how to properly use social media. Why is it, then, that most businesses still fail at social media marketing? Regardless of all the sources of information they have at their disposal, they still find it challenging to penetrate the social way of marketing their brands.

It might have crossed your mind to blame businesses for not putting in enough effort to advertise their brands. You may have also thought that businesses do not know what social media marketing entails. Interestingly though, most of them are well informed about digital marketing. So, what could be the real problem? To help you understand why most companies fail at social media marketing, we have done in-depth research for you. The following paragraphs will iron out for you some of the main reasons most businesses do not succeed in their marketing campaigns. Hopefully, you can learn from their mistakes and achieve success in your marketing endeavors.

No Strategy

The number one reason why most companies fail is because of their lack of a strategy to guide them in their marketing. A strategy is what defines your overall business goals when using social media as a marketing tool. The importance of having a strategy is that it links your plans to the goals you have set for your business. Equally, it drives you to meet those goals.

Bearing this in mind, working without a strategy would be similar to wandering in the forest without a map. Undoubtably, you will get lost. Most businesses simply think that social media marketing entails posting content on Facebook, Twitter, Instagram, and other platforms. Before even thinking about posting content on these pages, one should take a step back to determine what they wish to achieve.

Think about it this way - what would you like to achieve now that you wish to establish a social media presence? How are you going to achieve the goals you have set? Consider your resources; do you have sufficient resources to help you in meeting your targets? You should streamline everything before taking your first step in posting content on social media.

Don't assume that hiring a professional to do the job for you will be a good strategy; it is not. As the business owner, you must define your marketing goals and your plan of action to meet these goals.

Absence of KPIs

Key performance indicators will inform you of whether your business is headed in the right direction or not. After setting your goals, you should stop often and reflect on whether your strategy is working. If you don't have data analytic tools, how will you know that your business is growing? Simply looking at the increased number of likes on your social media pages does not necessarily imply that your business is doing well.

Most businesses end up adopting a winning mentality right

after seeing their followers increase or after noticing a sudden increase in viewership. Sure, numbers don't lie. However, you ought to make good use of performance metrics to gauge your social media presence. You also must ensure that not only are your followers and likes increasing, but your sales as well. Ideally, when you do this in the right way, you can determine whether your strategy is providing you with a competitive edge over your business rivals.

Lack of Consistency

Posting on social media networks inconsistently will also lead to frustration. Your marketing efforts will prove futile, because you will not see an increase in your engagement or number of followers.

People visit social platforms with the intention of interacting with others. By posting consistently, you increase the chances of gaining a wider reach. Also, you will boost your brand's awareness. Most of these platforms reward those who contribute on a regular basis.

Considering all the benefits of posting regularly on social networks, it is vital for you to maintain the pace. This is the only way you will attract a large following.

Focusing Too Much on Technology

The advent of new technologies has transformed how businesses operate. Unfortunately, most companies fail to understand that these technologies are there to help them serve their clients better. People are not interested to know whether or not you are using the latest technologies. They are more concerned about the problem you are solving. If you are not meeting their needs, then they will simply turn to your rivals for better customer service or improved products.

So, thriving in the business world is never about adopting the latest technologies. Rather, it is more about using these innovations to transform how you serve your clients. Don't get confused along the way.

Poor Choice of Platforms

Another common reason why most businesses fail is that they use a poor choice of social networks. Just because other businesses are winning customers through Facebook doesn't mean that you should also be on Facebook. Having an online presence with the best social media platform in the market today will not guarantee that your marketing campaign will succeed.

People have different reasons for utilizing separate social accounts. Therefore, your choice of social networks will also vary depending on the goals you wish to achieve. Your choice of social media platform can have a huge impact on your marketing strategy. If you make the wrong choice, you will end up spending a lot with little return in the end.

To ensure that you choose the best social networks, start by finding out more about your clients. Your target audience will determine where you should create an account. If most of your potential clients are on Pinterest, then it will make a lot of sense to have an account there instead of on Instagram. What you should bear in mind is that you are not creating an account for your personal needs. The social media account is meant to help you reach your target audience. So, first know where they are, then create the right account.

Lack of Resources

From what has been discussed so far in this book, it should be clear that promoting your brand on social media is not always easy. Marketing gurus will attest to the fact that running your marketing campaigns can be compared to a full-time job. You need to be there to respond to your customers, and to tweak your campaigns when necessary. Creativity is also required to guarantee that you create engaging content.

While creating an account on social networks is free, this doesn't necessarily mean that your marketing campaign will not cost you. For you to get the best results, you must spend money. It is important for you to pay for ads. Apart from this expense, you will likely have to dig deeper into your pockets to benefit from social media influencers. They will likely have a profound impact on your social media campaigns.

Sometimes you will also need the help of an expert to manage your marketing campaign. This will cost you money. Unfortunately, most business owners jump into the idea of social media marketing with the perception that they can market without any expense. Yes, this is possible, but you can rest assured that you will not get the best possible results.

Lack of Creativity

It takes a lot of effort to create engaging content on a regular basis. Truth be told, it is not an easy job. Most people who market their brands on social media run out of ideas. Running a successful campaign for two months is easy. However, maintaining the pace for a year or more will be a huge challenge. This is where your content marketing skills will be put to the test.

Crafting great content will require you to be informed about current and future social trends that have been discussed herein. You also need to gather a lot of information through extensive research. Sometimes, you will have to learn from what your competitors are doing.

Expecting Posts to Go Viral

Some businesses will fail in their marketing campaigns due to their high expectations. A huge number of new social media marketers will expect everything they post to go viral. Well, it should be made clear that going viral over the internet can mean a lot of things. For instance, your post could go viral for the wrong reasons. Therefore, when marketing your brand on social networks, the notion of expecting your posts to go viral should be erased from your mind. Simply focus on creating valuable content and post it to the right platforms; the social media network algorithm will do the rest for you.

The little mistakes that you make on your social media marketing campaign can cost you. For instance, failing to create a plan is planning to fail. Also, if you fail to measure your campaign's performance, then you are most likely headed for failure. Knowing why it is important for you to have an online presence is the first thing you should understand. Next, set clear tactics on how you will market your brand on different social networks. After that, you have to constantly evaluate your techniques to figure out if they are paying off. Most importantly, never forget to choose the right social platforms to suit your business.

Chapter 17: Proven Secrets to Increase Your Brand's Visibility on Social Media

One of the main reasons why businesses will turn to social media marketing is because they yearn to increase their brand's visibility. Without a doubt, companies post on social networks with the hopes of getting people to hear their message. However, a problem arises when no one is available to listen to what you have to say. In this case, regardless of how good your content is, your marketing efforts will not help you in any way.

Taking this into consideration, it is important for one to ensure that their social media posts are visible. Unfortunately, due to the existing algorithms on platforms like Facebook, it may not be so easy to gain the visibility you desire right away.

Luckily, there are numerous strategies you can adopt to help you increase the likelihood of your posts being seen by most people possible. The techniques discussed will aim to achieve the following:

- **Improve lifespan:** To guarantee that you make the most out of every post you share, it is vital to increase the lifespan of each post. This entails making sure that the posts gain and maintain popularity for a long time.

- **Maximize reach:** Of course, visibility means getting more people to see your posts. Therefore, it is crucial that you employ strategies that will maximize how many people you can reach with your posts.

- **Increase followers:** Looking at the bigger picture, your posts should gradually increase your following. A growing following will imply that your posts are visible to your audience. Moreover, if you are getting more followers every day, it shows that you are sharing valuable content.

So, what are the secrets to increasing your brand's visibility on social media?

Invest in Ads

Settling for free social media marketing strategies is a smart move for companies that are just starting out. However, this strategy is not nearly as effective as paid ads. The good thing about using paid ads is that they will easily reach your targeted audience due to the algorithm used by social networks.

Timing

Timing is another important consideration you should mull over. Yes, this tip might sound overrated, but it actually makes a lot of sense. If you post content at the wrong time, there is a likelihood that you will not reach your intended audience. Keeping in touch with your followers when they are most active on social media will definitely enhance your brand's visibility.

Likewise, you must time your posts to warrant that you share content when your competitors least expect it. Sharing your content when big players in the industry are also posting is not a brilliant idea. Most people will focus on posts from your rival brands if they have been in the market longer than you. Hence, you have to schedule your posts perfectly to increase your visibility.

Imagery

Most people will be lured in by multimedia content. Therefore, you should confirm that your posts feature appealing images. Try your best not to copy images from your competitors. The idea here is to stand out. Consequently, share unique images that will quickly grab your audience's attention.

Start Some Controversy

You can also make a bold move of sharing controversial posts. If you do this the right way, you will have people commenting about your message. At the end of the day, you will have made your brand more popular. When attempting this technique, you should be careful not to tarnish your company's image. You should not adopt unethical practices in the name of trying to capture your audience's attention.

Narrow Down Your Target Audience

It might sound strange that an ideal way of increasing your brand's visibility is through narrowing down your target audience, but this tactic works. This is because, by focusing on reaching the people who matter a lot to your business, you will increase the chances of getting the most out of them. In this scenario, there is a good chance that your audience will share your messages on their social media pages. Ultimately, you will have increased your visibility by only targeting individuals who have an interest in using the products or services you offer.

Be Diverse

Using the same ideas over and over again on your social media posts will only drive traffic away from your page. To grow your visibility, you should come up with new ideas. Give your audience something to look forward to. Combine this with the right timing, and you will surely make your brand visible.

Broaden Your Outreach

Getting your brand in front of a new audience is also an effective way of enhancing your social media presence. If you have been focusing on a particular location, you can expand your reach by sharing your promotional content with new customers. While doing this, you ought to confirm that your new audience features a group of people who are likely to depend on your brand or share your content.

Jump into Conversations

Another smart way of growing your social media presence is by getting into conversations that are ongoing. For instance, if there is an interesting interaction that is related to your brand, you can participate in such discussions. This technique works best when you know how to monitor particular keywords on social media networks. Also, you can track mentions using relevant hashtags. The benefit gained here is that the message will reach the people you wanted it to since they will already be talking about a problem or a solution that your brand can help them solve.

Stay Active

Having an inactive social media presence will certainly not get you the visibility you are looking for. You must keep your followers engaged with fresh content. To ensure that you stay active on different social media networks, try using automation tools. These will help you post content when you are not available. With the help of scheduling tools, you can simply spend a few minutes to organize content that will keep your audience talking about your brand. Remember that your presence will be complemented by the idea of scheduling posts at the right times.

Increasing your brand's visibility is what will keep people talking about your products and services. When posting content, it is imperative that you consider what your audience is after. Posting relevant information is what will make them want to like and share your content. Don't just post because you have a social media page. Post information when you are certain that your audiences are most active. This also helps to increase your visibility. Whatever you do to enhance your visibility on social media will also boost your campaign's effectiveness. Therefore, it is recommended that you stick with a plan that works for you.

Conclusion

Thanks for taking the time to read this book on social media marketing!

Hopefully you now have a good understanding of the different social media platforms you can use, and which ones might be best for your particular business.

Remember to always make a marketing plan that is specific to your business, and don't be afraid to try new things with your posting and advertising!

Thanks again for choosing this book. I wish you the best of luck in your business endeavors!

References

10 Insightful Twitter Statistics for Small Business. (2019, April 3). Retrieved from https://small-bizsense.com/10-insightful-twitter-statistics-for-small-business/

11 Companies That Are Killing It with Their Digital Marketing Campaigns. (2017, June 6). Retrieved from https://www.convinceandconvert.com/digital-marketing/killing-it-with-digital-marketing-campaigns/

11-Step Social Media Marketing Strategy That Works + [Free Template]. (2018, November 7). Retrieved from https://fitsmallbusiness.com/social-media-marketing-strategy/

15 Facebook stats every marketer should know for 2019. (2019, April 19). Retrieved from https://sproutsocial.com/insights/facebook-stats-for-marketers/

53 Incredible Facebook Statistics and Facts. (n.d.). Retrieved from https://www.brandwatch.com/blog/facebook-statistics/

Big Brands That Get Social Media Right. (2018, April 30). Retrieved from https://www.businessnewsdaily.com/10720-lessons-for-small-business-social-media-brands.html

DeMers, J. (2015, June 26). Top 10 Reasons Your Brand Needs To Be On Facebook. Retrieved from https://www.forbes.com/sites/jaysondemers/2015/06/26/top-10-reasons-your-brand-needs-to-be-on-facebook/

DePhillips, K. (2010, December 13). 18 Reasons Why Social Media Marketing Is Important For Any Business. Retrieved from https://www.contentfac.com/9-reasons-social-media-marketing-should-top-your-to-do-list/

Facebook owns a ton of popular apps, here are how a few big ones use your information. (2018, March 26). Retrieved from https://www.newsweek.com/facebook-own-instagram-does-companies-apps-data-860732

The Future of Social Media Marketing ? 11 Trends That Will Impact Your Business. (2019, May 13). Retrieved from https://shanebarker.com/blog/future-of-social-media-marketing/

Global social media ranking 2019 | Statistic. (n.d.). Retrieved from https://www.statista.com/statistics/272014/global-social-networks-ranked-by-number-of-users/

Hootsuite. (2019, January 23). 22 YouTube Stats That Matter to Marketers in 2019. Retrieved from https://blog.hootsuite.com/youtube-stats-marketers/

How to Start Using Instagram to Grow Your Small Business. (2018, December 31). Retrieved from https://www.quicksprout.com/2018/12/31/how-to-start-using-instagram-to-grow-your-small-business/

How to Start Using Instagram to Grow Your Small Business. (2018, December 31). Retrieved from https://www.quicksprout.com/2018/12/31/how-to-start-using-instagram-to-grow-your-small-business/

James A. Martin. (n.d.). 10 top social media marketing success stories. Retrieved from https://www.cio.com/article/3062615/10-top-social-media-marketing-success-stories.html

Joseph, J. (2016, May 10). 5 Successful Social Media Campaigns You Can Learn From. Retrieved from https://digitalmarketinginstitute.com/blog/5-successful-social-media-campaigns-you-can-learn-from

Reach vs Impressions: What's the Difference in Terms? (2018, February 15). Retrieved from https://sproutsocial.com/insights/reach-vs-impressions/

Twitter by the Numbers (2019): Stats, Demographics & Fun Facts. (2019, January 6). Retrieved from https://www.omnicoreagency.com/twitter-statistics/

What is social media marketing (SMM)? - Definition from WhatIs.com. (n.d.). Retrieved from https://whatis.techtarget.com/definition/social-media-marketing-SMM

www.ingramcontent.com/pod-product-compliance
Lightning Source LLC
LaVergne TN
LVHW011717060526
838200LV00051B/2927